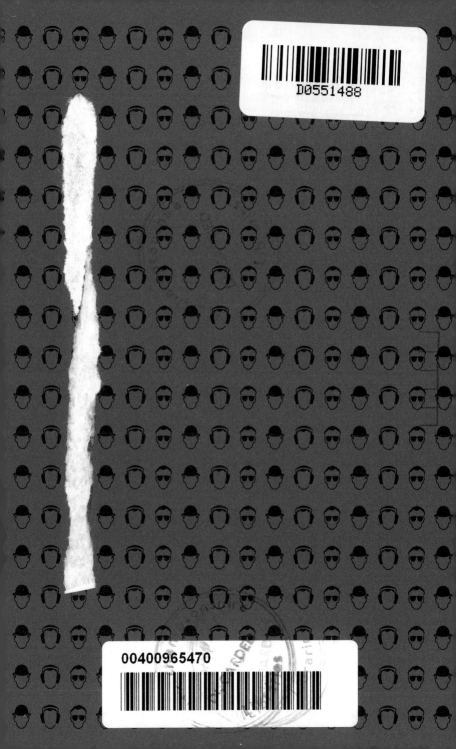

REAL MEN EAT PUFFER FISH

And 93 Other Dangerous Things to Consider

REAL MEN
Eat Puffer Fish
And 93 Other Dangerous Things to Consider

Robert Twigger

Weidenfeld & Nicolson

LONDON

To Rachel Barker and Clare Twigger-Ross

Acknowledgements

Ian Preece for sterling service above and beyond the call of duty. Natasha Fairweather for general acumen, support and generosity. Alex Hippisley-Cox for enthusiasm throughout many projects. The late illustrator David Graham, as well as Christopher Ross, always accurate in his notes, and always there.

First published in Great Britain in 2008 by Weidenfeld & Nicolson
an imprint of Orion Books Ltd
Orion House, 5 Upper St Martin's Lane, London WC2H 9EA

A CIP catalogue record for this book is available
from the British Library

ISBN 978 0 297 85438 8
Illustrations by David Graham
Printed and bound in Italy

In a strategy of sustainable development, this book is printed in the European
Community by L.E.G.O. Spa on Evviva 80gsm paper, made in Italy
following FSC standards, ensuring responsible managed forest.

Contents

1 Luis Bunuel's method for making a Dry Martini

The Dry Martini is a dying art form. Once the rocket fuel of 1940s and '50s New York, indeed half the civilised world, it is now relegated to cocktail bars where the waiters have to look up the instructions online while you wait drumming your fingers on the bar. The Dry Martini of Bond, by the way, is an abomination – vodka is inert in the presence of vermouth – you simply get a high-alcohol, spicy, sweetened wine, ideal for an alcoholic such as Ian Fleming whose liver needed clean vodka rather than devilish gin.

Bunuel, the surrealist film director who went on to make some of the most memorable films of the sixties, wrote in his memoir, *My Last Breath*, 'Considering the importance the Dry Martini has played in my life I shall devote at least four pages to it.'

What Bunuel recognised was that booze has its own alchemy. Getting toasted on San Miguel is different to hitting a single malt. Whereas rum may leave you feeling tight but alright, the same quantity of alcohol in a Brazilian Caipirinha may reduce you to a slobbering wreck. Champagne is, despite its detractors, capable of producing a rush to the brain, completely different to other wines. The particular carrier of the alcohol is all important. Vermouth, when mixed in almost homeopathic quantities with gin, in the presence of deep cold is transformed into something quite different from any of its constituents. It is a qualitative change: a new drink is made, rather as, when uranium is bombarded by atomic particles, a new element is formed. When you taste a true Dry Martini you understand at last its magical hold on generations of drinkers. How it lost that hold is also a mystery, maybe to be laid at the feet of Martini adverts that encouraged the drinking of vermouth without gin.

Bunuel recommends, first, that, like a good pastry chef, every item of Martini-making be cold, if not pre-frozen. Into a cold cocktail shaker filled with ice one pours a tiny quantity of Vermouth, no more than one-seventh of the quantity of gin one finally intends to use. He even suggests one-fifteenth the quantity – with Martinis, less is definitely more. Now stir – again Bond's gaucheness is revealed in his desire to have it shaken not stirred; shaking puts too much water into the drink. Then pour out the Martini quickly (any vermouth will do, Martini simply being the most well-known brand) and discard. Yep. Enough of what you need adheres to the ice cubes. Now pour in the gin together with four to seven drops of angostura bitters. These are not essential but they help bring out the flavour. Stir again, pour into an iced jug and serve.

Rocket fuel.

The effect of a correctly mixed Dry Martini is to launch one into a smooth reverie of all things that are fine and beautiful. In company, the conversation becomes expansive and yet precise – the very opposite of beer-fuelled babbling or the irritable loquaciousness of habitual red wine drinkers. Try it.

2 Build your own coracle

I was determined one recent summer to build a coracle, both to amuse my kids and to amuse myself. I had built one years before when I was fourteen. It was not entirely successful, but it did float. The secret I learnt was all in the bulge of the thing. If, sideways on, a coracle has the aspect of a saucer rather than one of those dumpy bottomed mugs, then you're in for a capsize. The coracle must bulge out at the waterline, or at least drop straight down before turning through a right angle to give a flat bottom to the boat.

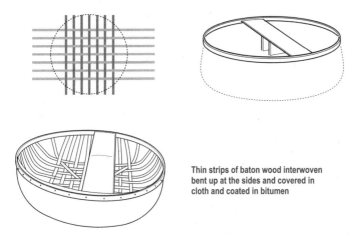

Thin strips of baton wood interwoven bent up at the sides and covered in cloth and coated in bitumen

The coracle is the traditional Celtic craft. They still ply in reduced numbers some of our western salmon rivers in Wales and Scotland. A few makers continue – usually making their craft from calico and tar, though the originals were made of cow, deer or horsehide – and the diminutive size of the boat is determined by the size of skin available.

My coracle design is dominated by ease of manufacture and speed of getting it onto the water. You want to get out there and hanging around knacker's yards waiting for old skins just takes too much time. The water calls. Also, there is considerable pleasure in making anything out of everyday objects. For your coracle nip down to the local DIY store and buy a pack of plastic cable ties (the sturdy kind), some garden twine, a cheap eyelet-making kit and, if they stock them, a heavyweight tarpaulin about three metres square. If you can't find such a strong tarpaulin there are several suppliers on the Net. You should be able to get one for under £15. You can use any kind of tarpaulin – a three quid one will work – but the stronger it is the less careful you have to be on root-infested riverbanks.

Next, head out to the river, motorway, bypass or nearest woods to get your sticks. Motorways with wooded sides are good places to cut sticks as no one ever stops and asks you what the hell you are doing. As long as you are a little bit hidden from the traffic, you can coppice the hazels and ash trees to your heart's content. You'll need about twenty whippy sticks two metres long, greenwood and bendy – preferably willow, but hazel or any wood that doesn't snap when you bend it will do. The diameter of the stick should be about two centimetres. Thick sticks can be split.

Stick the sticks upright in the ground in a pleasing oval shape about 1.75m by 1.5m. Weave more sticks in and out of the uprights to a depth of about 30cm. Then bend the sticks over, having softened them up in the steam of an electric kettle (on an extension lead from indoors). Use cable ties (three per stick) to join the bent-over sticks across the bottom of the boat. The bits that stick out around the side again soften in steam or hot water and poke down the basketweave around the sides.

Now secure the entire lower rim of the coracle with an inner and outer gunwale; that is, a continuous strip that runs inside and outside the lip of the boat to stop it collapsing. This is made with a longer stick, steamed if necessary and held to each upright with a cable tie. Trim all sticks and ties once that is done.

4

Use a knife to carve away any sticking-out sharp bits that might puncture the skin. Use duct tape to further soften sharp edges. Cover the coracle frame with the tarpaulin and mark roughly with a marker pen a line about 15cm down inside the coracle when the tarpaulin is folded over. Use the eyelet kit to make secure holes every 10cm around this line. Leave a further 10cm free and cut away the rest. Use the garden twine to lace the tarpaulin over the frame, tying it down from the eyelets to the frame.

Get a plank of wood with holes drilled either side and cable tie or U-bolt it across the gunwales (the edge of the top of the boat). This becomes the cross seat. Be careful about making holes in the tarp cover and secure any made using waterproof duct tape ironed on to make it stick better.

Buy an 'el cheapo' paddle or make one from a piece of plywood nailed to a thick, smooth stick (as smooth as possible otherwise blisters will appear).

Make a carrying strap of rope to hang the coracle over your shoulder. Head for the nearest water and make like an ancient Briton.

---

3 KGB technique for building up powers of intimidation

Are you ignored by waiters and singularly fail to catch the eye of taxicabs zooming by? Does a stern look at kids dropping litter merely elicit a few titters and even a rude remark or two? Do you find when telling someone off at work one's eyes are happiest elsewhere – looking away?

A powerful stare is an asset the KGB realised all agents should possess long ago.

At work in the seamy world of intelligence one needs powers of intimidation for use against intransigent couriers, undercover hotel staff, 'clean-up' men and other agents. At one's top-secret HQ one might need a little extra clout with colleagues, who may be about to cut into your budget for surveillance and dead-letter drops.

What better way than to utilise the KGB technique for building a truly intimidating stare. Readers of John le Carré will know that the KGB were never knowingly outstared. Look an agent in the eye and by golly you'll be the first to look away. Putin, we suspect, has outstared all his European counterparts despite his shifty looking exterior. Just what is their secret?

The Zoo.

Documented by defector Victor Suvorov in his book *The Aquarium*, Moscow Zoo was used as a handy place to nurture and perfect a seriously nasty stare. Normally one is a little nervous of turning the full beam onto a stray dog or even a cat with attitude, but zoos have bars. Lions usually engage for a while and then look away supremely bored. But for a moment there is a frisson of contact; the killer has looked into thy soul, so to speak. Really it's a whole new way of enjoying zoos, and as a bonus you can take the kiddies along, too. Wolves are quite good for a staring match, as are rhinos and crocs, though rhinos can go a bit crazy butting against the fence if they really don't like you. Horses and giraffes are good for practising what the Soviets termed 'the innate dominance of man over beast'. Well, you can try.

Small creatures like mongooses and meerkats can be surprisingly tenacious and refuse to be put off being eyeballed directly. Polar bears can hold a stare for ages, too; this is excellent training as a bear stare is particularly unnerving, especially if they charge at you, even if there are bars.

Monkeys, chimps, and the real score, giant gorillas, which, sharing so much of our genetic history, are naturally best suited to a staring competition. Gorillas can start to shout and beat their chests. Do not be put off. Keep staring until they blink and slope off to get more bananas. Baboons work too, but, failing to get into the spirit of things, can simply turn and show their red arses.

All in all, a few visits to the zoo will build a look guaranteed to burn holes in ice and send mere mortals running with its animal power and intensity.

Who stares, wins. Now, waiter, where's my bill?

4   A clever trick with a can of beans

It is late at night in your kitchen and friends are around.
Maybe it's the end of a party, perhaps the whiskey is
circulating. It is time for some kind of entertainment. Nothing
is better suited than trials of idiotic strength and bravery.
The can trick I picked up years ago from Anthony Greenbank,
noted author of the unique and dazzling (and authentic)
Mr Tough and the *Survival Handbook*, from whence it came.
Cans of beans look hard and strong. Indeed being whacked in
the face with one could cause serious injury. The very idea of
slamming a full can, unopened, onto one's unprotected digit
is enough to put anyone off, however tough they fancy
themselves to be. Of course there's a trick to it. Examine the
said can of beans and make sure the soldered seam is not
facing downwards. Make sure your finger lies extended onto
the tabletop alone with the other fingers curled back. When
you bring the can down do it as fast as you can and accurately.
You want an explosive smash, not something long and drawn
out. A slow delivery actually hurts more. Not that it will hurt
if you do it right. Slam the can down sideways (if end on you'll
cut the finger off) and the thin flesh of the finger will be
unharmed as the boniness of the digit dents the can. Don't
do it with coke cans.

5 How to cook and eat the deadly puffer fish

The puffer fish, or *fugu* as it is known in Japan, is a tropical fish that can inflate itself with water (or air if landed) to increase its size to scare off predators. It also has spines that contain poison and is itself highly toxic. Strangely, one of its main predators, the tiger shark, is immune to its poison, which in humans attacks the sodium content of nerve endings leaving one very quickly paralysed.

Even buying puffer fish is illegal in most European countries so you will have to go further afield. In Japan, whole puffers are not sold to the general public and the ones on display in Tokyo's Tsukiji fish market have already had their livers, the most poisonous part, removed. In Thailand, even though puffers have been illegal as a food product since 2002, it is quite easy to get one from local fishermen – if you dare. The closely related porcupine fish is also poisonous and is prepared in the same way.

Puffers are quite simply the most poisonous beasts on the planet. Tetrodotoxin, puffer fish poison, is 1,200 times more poisonous than cyanide and a typical fish contains enough of it to kill thirty people. In Japan there were 2,500 puffer fish deaths between 1945 and 1975. A crackdown on the sale of the fish to the public, plus stringent testing of would-be *fugu* chefs, reduced the death toll to a manageable five to ten a year in Japan with about a hundred cases of those poisoned actually recovering. Since 1958 the testing of puffer fish chefs has been compulsory. It's a tough test which involves cooking and eating a *fugu*, and only 30 per cent pass. Cooked and eaten *fugu* remains have been found in garbage pits over 2,300 years old. Though it's an ancient dish its dangers have caused it to be banned for centuries at a time. In the Tokugawa period (1600–1867), *fugu* consumption was illegal in the Tokyo area. There was also a partial ban in force during the Meiji period (1868–1912) and it is the only delicacy that is forbidden to the Emperor of Japan – even today.

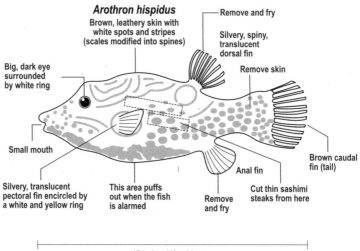

Arothron hispidus
Brown, leathery skin with white spots and stripes (scales modified into spines)

Remove and fry

Silvery, spiny, translucent dorsal fin

Big, dark eye surrounded by white ring

Remove skin

Small mouth

Brown caudal fin (tail)

Anal fin

Silvery, translucent pectoral fin encircled by a white and yellow ring

This area puffs out when the fish is alarmed

Remove and fry

Cut thin sashimi steaks from here

17 inches (43cm) long

The worldwide death toll is unknown – but do you want to be one of them? No, of course not, you just want to get a little high. This is the dirty secret of *fugu* – it's actually a rather bland fish unless you have traces of poison on your sushi or in your soup. Then your lips become comfortably numb and a strange euphoria takes hold. But steady on: if your tongue stops working and you start dribbling on your fellow eaters you may be in the first stages of tetrodotoxin poisoning for which there is NO KNOWN ANTIDOTE. You may then find your heart-rate going through the roof, feel dizzy, vomit, sense your blood pressure plummeting … without delay head for the nearest hospital and ask to be put on a ventilator as your lung muscles will soon be paralysed. Ingest charcoal to try and neutralise the poison – if you last twenty-four hours you should survive. Interestingly, puffer fish poison is used in Haiti to zombify people – it works to make you appear dead (paralysed with vital signs undetectable except by sophisticated equipment), but you can still see and hear everything.

You're still interested? Then first obtain a puffer fish – preferably a tiger puffer as they are the most toxic. The toxin is produced by bacteria living in the gut of the fish. If puffers are kept in freshwater aquaria for long enough and fed a non-seafood diet they begin to lose their toxicity. Having obtained your fish put on a pair of surgical gloves! Then using a razor-sharp *fugu* haki, or puffer fish knife (or a scalpel), open the fish carefully by slicing along its backbone and pulling back the spines and the skin to reveal the bone. Take care not to get spiked yourself. Pare the skin back to reveal the flesh on the flanks of the fish. Only remove these in wafer-thin slivers. Eat raw.

According to the Fugu Institute of Japan, 50 per cent of known cases of poisoning come from eating the liver, 43 per cent from ingesting the ovaries and 7 per cent from consuming the skin.

Eating only the flesh is the safest method. Avoid soups known as *chiri*, made from the entire fish, at all cost, even if the liver has been removed. Most poisoning comes not from raw *fugu* but from *chiri*. If you wish to eat more of the fish, fry up the fins in batter – very tasty.

If you choose to prepare the fish traditionally, open its guts very carefully and remove the liver, ovaries and heart with cautious knifework . Also remove the skin, the gills and the intestines. Again either fry up slivers of flesh or eat raw as sashimi or on rice as sushi.

Lastly, recall the words of the Japanese *haiku* poet Yosa Buson (1716–1783)

> *I cannot see her tonight*
> *I have to give her up*
> *So I will eat* fugu.

---

6 How to head-butt a block of ice in two

The head-butt is a bar-room manoeuvre par excellence – when space is cramped you can't swing a punch but you can nut someone.

By extension it seems a favoured tool of aggression by people who lived in cramped urban conditions, hence its euphemisms – the 'Glasgow Hello' and the 'Liverpool Salute'. The head-butt can be a shifty form of attack: you need to be up close to do it and sometimes artifice is used to get in range. Football players have a technical advantage because the line of bone where the forehead flattens out to become the crown is the edge used for heading and for the correct butt. It's actually the bony corner of the head that is used.

The Japanese have thinner bones, in general; you can see it in their narrower necks and wrists you can easily encircle in one hand. The great martial artist and founder of Aikido, Ueshiba Sensei, practised for hours as a young man head-butting trees wrapped once with a tight cord, known as a *makiwara*, and more usually used for toughening the knuckles of karate fighters. He knew there were situations where the head-butt is the unparalleled tool of aggression. If you are lucky enough to be inside someone's defensive range then a head-butt to the bridge of the nose, or lower, can end a fight before it has begun. The pain, the tears and the blood inflicted are often gratifying, or shocking enough (depending on your perspective), to make one a confirmed head-butter for life.

Women, in general, avoid the head-butt. It is a masculine manoeuvre. In the case of skinheads, the simple removal of their hair is a tacit preparation of the head prior to the butt. Perhaps the tattooing of 'SKINS' or 'Made in Britain' on the forehead is an attempt to turn the head into not just a weapon but also a stamp, a unifying stamp that leaves its mark on others.

To someone who wishes to build head-butt power, a certain amount of training is required. Primarily one is building strength and coordination in the neck muscles and using not just the weight of the head – which is considerably more than a hammer, more like a mini-sledgehammer – but following through, adding to the natural momentum of the head-butt rather in the way you accelerate a swing by timing your push exactly as the swing passes. The strongest head-butt, and you can see this in any football game where a long header is made, utilises the strength of the entire body. It is not merely a wobbling of the heavy head, but a slight flexibility of neck allied to the upper body moving forward from the waist. The head's movement merely initiates the move; the real force travels up in a straight line through the back from the backside. That is why head-butting trees should be done lightly – only people and things that will shatter should meet with the full weight of the body transmitted through the ridgeline of the skull.

Done right, you should not even feel jarred; done wrong and you'll get brain damage. You can get a feeling for the right and perfect striking area by hitting yourself like Basil Fawlty repeatedly with the hard heel of your hand. Do that enough and you will habituate the part of your head that is ripe for butting; you will find by default the sweet spot so to speak. Then practise initiating the move in a continuous line from the tailbone to the forehead, with the whole line of your self moving forward in attack. That should do it.

Now to the business of breaking the ice with one's nut. The first and biggest part of this trick is to know that there is a trick to it. We'll get to that in a minute. The second is practising the head-butt without braining yourself. Start easy, by holding a cushion over a book and bringing one's head down hard. Bringing the book up a fraction helps too, as this leads to the main part of it, which is the trick. Breaking a plank of wood either by a punch or a kick is easy enough with practice. To break a brick or a block of ice is not – they are simply too massive. But like tearing the phonebook in two, the trick is everything. The block of ice is not suspended, as the plank is, across a gap for ease of breaking. The weakness of a plank lies in the leverage one can exert on its central point. For the ice block, being thick, this is not the case (thin ice, true,

can be treated like glass, but that is hardly impressive).
The ice block and the brick are broken best through sudden
shattering. One corner of the block is raised up by the fingers.
This does not need to be surreptitious. In fact one can even
hold the entire block an inch but no more above the breaking
surface – a marble kitchen top or a solid oak table would be
best. You then bring the head down to hit the ice and as you
hit you drop the ice, or let it slide, from your grip; the fall,
added by the power of the head's swing, causes the ice block
to shatter, hopefully to great applause.

7 How to land a 747 jumbo jet

The jumbo jet has been in service for nearly forty years and
in its latest form, the 747–8, is still being made. There are
hundreds in service and if an accident befalls you in the air
it is quite likely that you will be aboard a 747. Suspend
judgement for a moment and imagine the following scenario:
terrorists have wangled their way through lax customs in
Punto Arenas in Chile and have, over the Amazon, wrested
control of the 747 flight you are on to Mexico City – why isn't
important. Then the terrorists fall out and after a mighty
bloodletting with plastic airline cutlery no one is left alive on
the flight deck except a screaming stewardess. Though there
are several qualified heart surgeons on board there isn't a
single pilot, amateur or otherwise. Things get worse – though
the plane is still on autopilot the terrorists have smashed the
radio, so there is no chance of being 'talked down'.

So it's all down to you.

First – regret all the time you could have learnt exactly what to do by flying the many easily available flight simulators that run on ordinary PCs, some available as free downloads from the Net. Too bad. The next regret is that you're going to crash. Yes, accept that you will crash and what follows will be much easier to handle. But it will not be a fatal catastrophic crash; it will merely be a crash-landing, which we hope all passengers will walk away from just a little bit shaken.

Flying planes is easy, flying them well is hard. The good news is that, unlike a helicopter, an aeroplane as good-natured as a jumbo jet is inherently stable. You have to screw up very badly to make it do something dangerous and unexpected. Jumbos, especially when nearly empty of fuel and cargo, have very low stall speeds – just above 100mph when flaps are up and wheels are down. That should be a comforting thought; why, it's even on the scale of driving a car.

OK – you are going to have to fly this plane to somewhere you can land. You have two choices: the sea or a motorway. The sea is usually fatal so let's pick a big road. With a top pilot and a lightly loaded plane a jumbo can land in under a mile of road. You should allow for two or three – and the straighter the better. What about telegraph poles and other obstructions? Well, the fewer of these the better. Hitting one as you land will result in a bad crash, but not necessarily a fatal crash. You might even get lucky and find an airfield or even an airport. So, engaged in the gruelling task of looking out of the window, first identify your landing strip. Next, switch off the switches labelled autopilot A and autopilot B.

A jumbo will glide for twenty minutes even with its engines off. That's a long time when everyone in economy is screaming. But you have engines – all four. You should set the speed to around 150 nautical miles per hour and set the rate of descent to no more than five times this amount in feet – so around 600 feet per minute should be fine. Move the thrust levers until you get the speed you want – check the airspeed

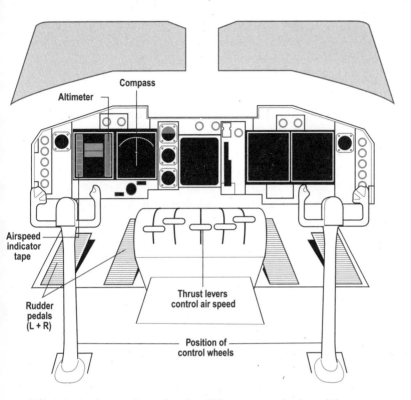

Altimeter

Compass

Airspeed
indicator
tape

Rudder
pedals
(L + R)

Thrust levers
control air speed

Position of
control wheels

dial right in front of you for that. Then move the joystick
('spectacles' they call them in the trade) forward gently until
the rate of descent registers. The great thing about flying even
a big plane is that you feel resistance through the controls.
This tells you if you are doing something too harshly. Level
off at around 2,000ft and start looking for somewhere to land.

To turn right move the rudder bar at your feet to the right –
do this gently. Also you can bank the plane while turning to
make it easier: do this by leaning the joystick also to the right.
Now you can move you can inspect where you will land.

Quickly check the fuel levels on the flight engineer's side
(look for the labels). A 747 drinks about a gallon a second,
so allow 3,600 gallons per hour of flying.

17

Once you have identified a long strip of clear land – wide, open road or airport – line yourself up, preferably heading into the wind – check the air direction indicator for this. If you can't land into the wind, don't worry.

Make several passes sighting up the beginning of the landing strip from as far away as you can. Line everything up so that you only have to manage descent speed and airspeed. On the final line up lower the undercarriage and set the flaps to full.

Keep the start of the landing strip lined up with your direction from the compass and alter your descent speed and airspeed to keep it level. Set the thrust on the engines to idle and see what the speed levels out at. If it is around 120–130 nautical miles per hour that should be fine; now move the stick forward to set a rate of descent to no more than 500–600 feet per minute – which will take four minutes from 2,000ft to landing. Four minutes is about ten miles away from the strip, so this should be your rough starting point.

Set the auto-brakes.

Keeping it all lined up, do not attempt to 'land'. You are going to try and get as low as possible and simply fly along the ground and by touching the ground you will have landed. Then, by applying brakes and reverse thrust (which is just directing the jets' force against forward movement) you will slow to a stop.

As you approach, level off the descent speed so that you are flying over the ground – hopefully it will seem very close. When the altimeter registers 50ft pull back on the stick to 'flare' the plane a little and not dig the nose in, but not so hard that you start to rise again.

When you hit the ground, keep it straight using the rudder bar and press the toe brakes on the bar. Get your flight assistant to push the thrust into reverse thrust position.

Wait for the plane to coast to a halt and listen for the cheers of all the people you have saved. Descend using the inflatable mattresses, sliding on your backside, briefcase on your lap and a big smile across your face.

---

8 How to fight a duel

Duelling has long been illegal and unfashionable in most countries around the world, but not all. In Paraguay it is not a criminal offence to fight a duel as long as both parties are registered blood donors; so the first step for any latter-day duellist is to buy a one-way ticket to Asuncion, Paraguay's capital or, if feeling confident, a return.

Duelling began as a simple way of settling disputes where there were no witnesses and less law. It developed into a highly codified way of preserving face, dignity and reputation. But in a world where shame and honour meant increasingly little, duelling fell into rapid decline. The last duel fought in Canada, in Newfoundland in 1873, is somehow symptomatic: one of the protagonists fainted before the first shot was fired and in the camaraderie of revival both agreed it was a nonsensical thing to do in the first place. So duelling died out. The Russians kept it up longest in Europe and after that it was only the Latin Americans.

In 1952, Senator Allende, later president of Chile, fought a duel with his colleague Raul Rettig, later to be Brazilian ambassador. Duelling was already illegal in Chile by this time, but only one shot per man was fired and both failed to hit their target.

Even as late as 1960 when a blind Borges was lecturing in

Argentina he challenged some hectoring students to a knife duel outside. They declined sheepishly and the author was hustled out of the building by his minders.

It is interesting that Paraguay, considered one of the least civilised of South American states, with its record of inordinate and wasteful wars against all its neighbours, has kept duelling longest.

If two people want to take pot shots at each other they might like to be reminded of the last duel in Scotland between a bank manager and a grocer – the bank manager was ex-army and an expert shot; the grocer a novice. The grocer shot and killed the expert.

And so to weapons. Abraham Lincoln once fought a duel with the choice of weapons his (the challenged always gets to choose) and chose cavalry broad swords, a weapon naturally suited to such a tall man. He won. There is something not quite right about such an eccentric weapon, though. It smacks too much of wanting to win. This may sound obtuse, but if winning was what it was all about then duelling would never have survived. There has to be a little give and take on both sides; honour demands that you give your opponent a fighting chance.

Before taking that trip to Paraguay, however, it might pay to study the rules of duelling or the *codo duello*.

1 The offence, usually a lie, slander or insult to a lady, is answered by a challenge. There is no slapping of faces with gloves, simply a thrown-down gauntlet. In some countries, Ireland and England, gentlemen did not hit each other (they only fought with swords), whereas in Europe one might slap the face of the man who insults you.

2 The man challenged can publicly apologise or make some other form of restitution of honour. If not he chooses weapons.

3 The challenger can then choose the location: the so-called

'field of honour'. If the challenged man is a crack shot, one might try to even the odds by choosing a bizarre field of honour, such as wearing skis on a snowy slope. Reputedly a pistol duel was fought from two gas balloons in nineteenth-century France.

4 Arrive with seconds – at least one, but three per side is the traditional number – and a doctor. The seconds must try to settle the argument peaceably, but if they fail the duel is on. Seconds must also keep an eye on cheating. An honourable second has been known to shoot his own man for cheating.

5 In a sword duel a square twenty paces by twenty paces is marked out with coloured silk handkerchiefs. To leave this space is considered cowardice.

6 The duellers agree to fight until a certain condition is fulfilled, usually until one side is too wounded to continue or the doctor has called proceedings to a halt. Early duelling manuals decry as weak the policy of the winner being the one who draws first blood.

7 If pistols or other weapons are used, the rules change somewhat. The challenged, after naming his weapon of choice can have it refused by the challenger. He must name another weapon until the challenger is satisfied.

8 The challenged chooses the place, the challenger the number of paces. An ultra-serious affair – five paces. Normal is ten paces. Honourable is twenty. Fifty is purely for show.

9 If pistols are the weapons of choice, the challenged gets the first shot. The order and style of firing has to be agreed. On a word or signal or 'at leisure'.

10 After two shots each, the seconds are bound to intervene and ask if the matter is settled. Otherwise more shots are fired until someone's aim is affected by a wound, or death, which signals the end of it.

11 If ultra serious the seconds can take over and fight too.

12 The doctor's fee is paid for by the challenger.

So there you have it: book your flight to Paraguay, register yourself as a blood donor and fight your duel.

---

9 How to punch without breaking your wrist

Every man should be able to punch, or rather, everyone does punch something or someone at some stage, even if it's just a wall or a door made out of surprisingly strong plywood. Fences too can look flimsy, but in a fit of rage or lamentable drink-fuelled elation or aggression one can easily bust a wrist in such casual acts of wanton destruction. Mark, too, the occasions of righteous anger where honour demands results in throwing a punch years after one thought one was far too old for such shenanigans. The following scenarios: it is your eighteen-year-old daughter's first real (i.e., drink-fuelled) party. You are the unofficial bouncer. The ugly and uninvited arrive. You bar their entry and they are unhappy. If, say, some young thug tries to land one on you and you punch back after having imbibed copious quantities of cider or alcopops, it would be a double disaster to also break your wrist. Or perhaps you are surprised by your wife running off with another man; again a punch might seem inevitable and no doubt years later when your children relate the event you will appear heroic if perhaps hot-headed, but if the wrist is broken the whole point of the thing will seem a tad retarded.

Young men are neither as strong nor as determined as old bruisers. They also have more flexible tendons. Add these two together and you get the likelihood of a wrist or hand fracture increasing with age. UNLESS you have learnt how to punch. Without gloves.

Boxing is an admirable art, but not better training for learning to punch than smacking what the Japanese call a *makiwara*. You can make one in about ten minutes. Just find a plank of wood or a small tree and wind it round and round with rope – natural hairy rope not polypropylene. Then get a felt tip marker and colour in the flat face of your knuckles. Then punch. If an area larger than the two-inch square formed by your first and second finger knuckles and the first finger joint is imprinted then you are not focusing the punch (see diagram).

Keep practising and thinking of your punch as a delicate weapon and not a ham-fisted walloper. A punch is not a push as the late great Bruce Lee once said and practical physics tells us the smaller the area of contact the greater the pressure.

And damage. Mostly people punch too hard. That doesn't mean you should pull your punches, but it does mean that you shouldn't be surprised if you break jaws, noses, teeth and … wrists. By using the square of two inches you will automatically line up the force of the punch with the centreline of the wrist. This means it won't flip over, which also means you won't break your wrist.

Attend to your *makiwara* daily. If you can fix the padded plank in a place you pass constantly – behind a door to the loo, your bedroom or office – then you can get into the habit of loosing off a swift left and right as a kind of physical toll to be charged on entry. By such effortless means can a punch be developed which may never be tested but at least is nothing to be ashamed of.

As to style of punching there are various well-known shots – uppercut, straight right, left hook etc. All tend to merge in the fury of ill-considered violence. It is best for the casual amateur of pugilism to leave fancy combinations to the likes of Sylvester Stallone; the main thing to avoid is the haymaker, the swinging favoured shot of the drunkard; originating behind the ear, one swings in an arc rather than a straight line. Sometimes they connect and work, often they do not and the combination of curve and power means the likelihood of a wrist fracture caused by the wrist toppling over on impact is increased. The deadly straight central line punch is best. You only need to master one type of shot and standing in line behind elbow, wrist and fist lines up the forces for an uncomplicated unleashing of violence.

To normalise punching in your home hang a heavy punch bag from one of those expandable chin-up bars you can buy in Argos. Put the chin bar across the door frame leading to your bedroom/study/garage and give the bag a hefty whack as you pass.

Kung fu men like to practise chain punching, a bit like punching as if one's hands are peddling a cycle. It is a good way to build speed and stamina and again, hitting down the central line is both quicker and less complicated.

24

More often one is tempted to punch a wall than a person. In a moment of supreme exasperation, perhaps when one is woken for the fifth time of a night with a newborn infant and it's 'your turn'. Do not become the laughing stock of your friends and family by aiming an ill-made punch at your house's hardwood interior; instead, through practice, unwind at your punch bag or *makiwara* with skill and confidence and expurgate those inner demons.

10 Casanova's thirty-three rules of rapid seduction

Casanova famously declared that he could bed most women he met within fifteen minutes, including nuns. He had some massive failures with younger damsels who led him astray, but in general his record was nothing short of impressive. He was also famously ugly and possessed a penis of less than normal length and girth. What then was his secret? Of course, some things may have changed since the eighteenth century, but not *everything*.

1 The stand. Simply stand behind the chair of a beauty besieged by suitors. Say nothing. Your presence will be sensed and the suitors will depart, driven away by your commanding presence. Eventually the beauty will have to turn to you and by default she will be yours.

2 Invite women to go on exceedingly long walks in the country. Opportunities will assert themselves.

3 Assume the commanding position with the skilful laying on of hands – offer to cure aches and pains by the massage of their calves and knees. Avoid the neck and shoulders as these provoke fear of strangulation in all females. Avoid the

feet, unless the situation is one where your own feet are also bare.

4   Speak and joke without any semblance of desire.

5   Find by deceit their birthday. Make a skilful pretence at guessing their astrological sign. Use this to make vague flattering guesses about their innermost self. Remember, all people desire heart-to-heart connection with others and that they fear rejection, snobbery and being used in some way.

6   Be genuinely interested but offer no advice.

7   At every meeting offer a dry hand, a kind smile and a thoughtful gift that flatters her vices or reminds her of her childhood.

8   Be completely at ease.

9   Say nothing, just look into their eyes while reciting inwardly the twelve times table.

10   Remark on how much you admire women writers, especially women biographers and hagiographers.

11   Ascertain whether they are married, single or engaged. Proceed to make unflattering comments about the state they do not inhabit.

12   Talk with pride about your father and encourage them in father worship, too.

13   Offer to hypnotise them. Do it. When they are 'under' make admiring but highly personal comments.

14   Offer to paint them in the nude. Make an appointment.

15   Contrive to meet them in a brand-new red-painted chariot or carriage.

16   Concentrate your attentions on women leaving places of dance instruction, long church services and the care of horses.

17 Wear one item of clothing that is superlative – either shoes or silken neck tie – and capitalise on its attraction powers.

18 Offer to read her pulse in the 'Chinese Style'. This means taking into account its regularity and variable strength. Deliver a verdict that reveals she dislikes false friends and desires to meet someone who really understands her innermost heart.

19 Tell her sincerely when one item of clothing is wrong.

20 Engage women in talk around the sweating hindquarters of horses.

21 Demonstrate that all dogs and cats and babies love you instinctively by dousing your hands in liquorice water.

22 Copy a beautiful poem by an obscure master and leave it in a prominent position only when a lady is in two minds whether to be seduced or not. A man capable of such fine feeling cannot be a monster, or so her reasoning goes.

23 Be not an audience but rather a sympathetic presence.

24 For the moment they are with you use every worn-out method to make them feel they are the most important thing in your life. Find by relentless questioning that which is within them that genuinely interests you. From this slim start enlarge your interest to the whole. Likewise with aspects of their physiognomy.

25 Assume in the first instance the manner of an aesthete – effete, artistic, voluble and pliable.

26 Assume in the second instance the silent manner of a murderer, thickset with heavy hands.

27 Assume in the third instance the manner of a sculptor transfixed and fully engaged in his task.

28 Allow rumours of your dalliance with others to spread, include rumours of whoring, too.

29 Seduce older women with direct and playful reference to the pleasures of the flesh.

30 Set out your stall even though it may be shunned. Elicit anger over some tiny disagreement. Then walk away. Arrive then powerfully on neutral ground and in a most lordly way be seen to arrive at a higher and better understanding.

31 Offer hope.

32 Convey in all its splendour the way of the world and show with skill your mastery thereof. Then use drink to work its insidious magic.

33 Be an uninvited guest. Overstay your welcome. Fall asleep at the hearth at a late hour. Prowl through the house looking for half-open doors.

11 Tracking for townies

Tracking is first and foremost about familiarity. Just as a DJ can guess an entire song from the opening thirty seconds, so too can a tracker visualise a scene from a few hoof prints and bits of broken grass. Both can do it because they are so familiar with the world they inhabit. If you only go into the wilds infrequently then you will never learn to track. You have to spend days there, eventually seeing the animal you wish to track actually making the track and then you have a benchmark from which to move – a pristine, brand-new track which you know for certain was made by the animal you just observed. Even while living in a town, you can improve your chances of learning by raking a patch of ground clear of any debris. It helps if it is sandy and close to water, which is a major convergence point for most animals. You can use this cleared ground for capturing the tracks of any passing animals.

When you find a track clue, be it a footprint or scuff marks on the ground, it pays to stop, look, listen and smell – for ages if necessary. Tracking is a good way to get into a Zen-like frame of mind. Don't lose this track clue until you find the next clue, even if it takes two hours. As long as you don't give up, the time taken will move your tracking skill up a level. If nothing is immediately visible, move in a series of fanning arches to see if you can find something. Remember, just like in *The Shining*, an animal can backtrack and turn off some way before the seeming endpoint of a trail. This explains those mysterious tracks that suddenly seem to vanish into thin air.

Don't lose that last clue as this is your reference point. Mark it with a piece of tissue paper, and if you go a long way from it make a tissue trail – single sheets biodegrade rapidly even if you leave them. If fanning arches fails to uncover the animal's trail, walk in an ever-widening spiral until you find the next track clue. Walk alongside what you perceive as the animal trail so you don't damage it.

To see things from an animal's perspective, get down on your hands and knees and look around. Animals tend to circle objects they find suspicious, so look for that circling tendency. Animals who rely on scent often keep their noses to the wind in order to sniff predators ahead. As the wind changes, so does their path. Watch out for the 'J'-hook move where an animal will proceed in a series of linked 'Js', hooking back on itself and pausing before moving on again.

Look at everything along the track – broken grass stems, bits of discarded wool – and also take into account the lie of the land in order to guess the direction the animal is running in.

Examine any dung you come across to get an idea of what the animal is eating. Knowledge of this will help you find where they like to go and where they have been. Dead animals, if you can stomach it, carry evidence of their food inside them; it may be partially digested, but it is still recognisable.

Bear in mind that all tracking is easiest first thing in the morning, especially if the dew has been disturbed. Even if there is little dew, the slanting morning light catches broken twigs and bits of torn fur much more easily. Always view a potential trail by looking into the sun as small dents and disturbances show up much better that way.

Should the animal be wounded, blood trails can be followed with a spray of hydrogen peroxide, which produces a bluish luminescence on dried bloodstains that lasts about forty-five seconds. This helps distinguish them from dried mud.

Read all you can about the animal that interests you. Extra information always helps with interpreting the clues you find.

Interpreting the age of tracks is again just a matter of having seen enough tracks being made and then coming back each day to see how they have changed. In the desert I followed a lizard track and saw its clear trail suddenly become vague after a spot where the lizard's body imprint was clear. The story was obvious: the lizard had slept there overnight – the clear tracks were him leaving that morning, the dulled ones the effect ten hours of light breeze had had in levelling the sand.

Reading human tracks to identify heights and limps and physique is easiest to learn by walking with people across the beach or somewhere that is consistently muddy. Watch how each body type walks and then compare that to the track they make. Photograph the track each type makes and compile a Sherlock Holmes-type dossier on the subject. You can also do this with horses and dogs in order to make stunning conclusions for all to admire while out on country walks.

When tracking vehicles, be they cars, motorbikes or cycles,

obey the same principles: observe the actual vehicle making a track, examine that track, remember it in detail and then apply it to unknown tracks you meet at a later stage. Guessing tyre track age becomes easy in the desert once you have been there a while and know how the weather has been for the last few days (a strong breeze can bury tracks in hours). Guessing the direction is not always so easy. Look for where the vehicle has gone over a bump – there will be a flattening out of the tyre immediately after this. Stones that have been dug in and then thrown back by the spinning wheels also indicate direction.

Tracking people across patches of car park and then back into the woods, as FBI trackers are prone to do, is actually mostly inspired guesswork. You line up the track already followed and project a likely course across the track-free area. You can then pick up the track on the other side.

One old technique is to match your stride length to that of the person tracked. Carry a stick and get into a rhythm of tapping at every point where there should be a right footprint. As you cross seemingly trackless tarmac or rock, examine every point at which you tap minutely. You may well discover micro disturbances, shards of mud or displaced granules of sand that indicate the man walked this way. This works for a straight track but, as reason suggests, there is no way to track along twisting streets unless you're a bloodhound or a KGB agent. One of their endlessly sly and inventive (and eventually lethal) techniques for tracking a would-be defector across an urban landscape was to dust their shoes with radium or any other radioactive material. The tracking agent would then follow at a discreet distance with a Geiger counter.

12 Poaching

Poaching is one of the great pleasures of life and one that in the past was often punishable by death. Such severity was a mark of how much the landowner valued the closely allied pleasure of hunting. Poaching adds to that pleasure the frisson of lawbreaking, but of a recent law, the ownership of land – how can anyone own land? It is an abomination: all poachers are anarchists at heart.

Poaching is a kind of Robin Hood activity. It is stealing, but from the rich. Of course many poachers are scumbags who steal pheasants and salmon to make a pretty profit, but these are poor representatives of the poacher's art. Salmon poaching was once such big business the great estates would employ ex-SAS men to guard their rivers. Salmon is so cheap now that river poaching is hardly a problem. Pheasants are poached, but again, commerce makes it an unprofitable game. Poaching has returned to its roots, which is a yeoman art devoted to undermining the inequality inherent in landownership. That's how I see it anyway.

Good poachers walk in the woods and fields almost every day. They know the land better than the farmer or the 'real' owner. By seeing farmland and woodland change slowly throughout the year you really understand it. You know where the game are likely to be and at what time. Very early in the morning, before dawn, is a good poaching hour, though not so popular as the hour just before darkness falls. Early has the advantage that the farmer, if up, will be busy with cows. Along the fragrant hedgerows you creep, armed with a silenced shotgun or an air rifle with a folding stock. Powerful silenced air pistols aren't bad either. One of the great things about shooting at dusk is the odd acoustical quality of the air – a shot fired cannot be traced accurately; the sound seems to come from all sides.

For those who prefer total silence there is surreptitious snaring (set the snares in the evening and collect at dawn) or using raisins soaked in strong alcohol. Pheasants love raisins and the alcohol is supposed to knock them out, though this might need fine tuning. Polish spirit, an extra-strong vodka, might prove best. Roald Dahl promoted the idea that leaving paper cones seeded with raisins and liberally smeared inside with glue would work to catch pheasants. Pheasants, like chickens, become passive in the dark. With their head glued in a cone the passive pheasant is pocketed by the pleased poacher. More realistically one can throw a net over pheasants eager for their raisins. Go nightly and prepare them, perhaps leading them by a trail of raisins to a place where you can drop the net unobserved from above.

Other pheasant pleasantries include shining a torch into a tree where they roost: thus startled, your accomplice can then sneak up behind and grab them by the legs or club them down and then bag them. This one sounds difficult.

Fish poaching is best done in the dead of night using a net. Yep. Sport is out. Get a 'survival' fishing net from the States by mail order or from Sweden – they're illegal and despised here in Britain. Stretch the net across a stream and see how much you catch in a night. If you need floats, small mineral water bottles work. Weights can be lead or stones in plastic bags.

A long-line baited with worms is pretty nifty. Attach twenty or so short leaders with hooks to a long line and let that go with the flow in the river. Recover your catch at dawn.

Salmon and trout congregate in pools beneath waterfalls, taking a rest before leaping up. Two men in chest waders with a net can close in and bag them. If you fall over make sure air trapped in your waders doesn't keep you under water.

Many landowners and gamekeepers are lazy folk and creatures of habit. Learn their habits and outwit them. Contract gamekeepers are really just pheasant feeders these days, putting out the feed so the corporate clients can get a good bag at the weekend. They love their Land Rovers and quad bikes: exploit this mechanised laziness to go off the beaten track. If surprised, leg it along a route where the gamekeeper must also run to follow you.

The above information is supplied for research purposes only and in no way condones the illegal trapping, shooting and killing of innocent animals owned by wealthy people. Just so you know.

---

13 Be a wheel-well stowaway

Stowing away in the undercarriage of a Boeing 747 or a big Airbus is a favoured technique for escaping the Third World and other places people are not always allowed to leave. For the desperate or the risk-taker it is a very cheap flight, though highly risky, mainly because of cold and lack of oxygen. A plane can fly for hours at 39,000ft – higher than Everest and you'll have no time to acclimatise. But people have made it; young and thin people tend to do better at surviving, and shorter flights are always to be preferred. In 1986, a thirty-five-year-old man, clad only in baseball cap, thin shirt and trousers, survived a two-and-a-half-hour flight in the wheel-well of a Boeing 707 from Panama to Florida at 39,000ft with temperatures outside as low as −63°C.

The tyres and the hydraulics provide some warmth –

especially at the beginning of the flight. To be safe, though, you better wear exceptionally warm clothing – several layers of wool, moon boots lined with straw or special insulating socks, a down jacket and trousers. Bring along several flasks of piping hot cocoa to help keep your spirits and core temperature up.

Wearing all that gear might hamper an unobserved dash for the undercarriage. That, too, is essential, as no pilot is keen on having stowaways. However, if you make it to the underside of the plane, climb up the tyre and the strut (quite easy this) and into the bay. Avoid the nose-wheel, which has less space as several crushed stowaways have discovered. The wing wheel-wells are the usual refuge. The DC8 *right* wheel-well has a space about a cubic metre – big enough for two small adults; the *left* wheel-well, on the other hand, is full of hydraulics and has no space at all. The 707's left wheel-well has been used, as have both sides of a 747. You can actually see from the ground if there is space extending back into the wing, a kind of ledge area which is unaffected by the raised wheels. You might also check the fuselage wheel-wells on a 747, which have lower struts to climb.

Once you are snugly ensconced in your bay, wait for take-off. When the wheels are up you'll feel warm for a while, but it will soon get icy cold. Oxygen will get scarcer and ideally you should have brought along a canister or two of pressurised oxygen as used by paramedics or climbers. With judicious application you can remain conscious on a shorter flight. If you have no oxygen then you have to trust to the body's own defences of hypothermic and hypoxic shutdown. Basically, the lack of oxygen and extreme cold send the body into a kind of hibernation that can result in brain damage, but not in every case. As the plane comes in to land, the increasing warmth and air revive the stowaway and he has to be ready to brace himself so as not to fall from the open wheel-well.

That's your final challenge – not falling like a frozen chunk of meat onto the runway at 150mph. You might consider packing a climbing harness to clip yourself to the top of the wheel strut, so that even if you are unconscious you don't fall just before landing. It's probably a good idea to wear a crash helmet, too …

14 Lessons for shipwrecked souls and castaways

Being shipwrecked is never a very pleasant experience, but with judicious preparation you can make the most of it and, more importantly, survive!

Firstly, there is a high chance that you will live. You are surrounded by water and food and if you have an EPIRB emergency beacon help may already be on its way. If not, take inspiration from the exploits of Poon Lim, a Chinese sailor, who, in 1942, survived 130 days adrift in the Atlantic on a wooden palate raft using a bent nail and a piece of unravelled string to catch fish. For water he relied on whatever rain he could capture using his lifejacket.

Let us imagine your luxury cruise ship in the Bahamas has just struck a rogue floating mine left over from the Second World War, or your chartered sailing yacht has been treated to the mating ritual of the great grey whale – whatever your starting point you are now alone in the ocean in a tiny rubber raft with very little food or water.

One thing worth packing on such voyages is a blow-up solar still. This device is like a see-through inflatable cone and produces more than a litre of fresh water a day from saltwater. Cheap and reliable, it will keep you alive.

Assuming you have very little survival equipment then you must trust to the experiments of French survival expert Dr Alain Bombard, who crossed the Atlantic alone in 1952 on a rubber raft with no food and water. He subsisted entirely on seawater, fish juice, rain and raw fish he caught using a gaff made from a bent penknife blade.

Bombard had *les grands bals*, as the French say, and when people questioned his ideas about sucking juice out of fish and drinking seawater he set out to sea to prove them all wrong. His first major discovery was that you can drink up to 0.8 litres of seawater a day without ill effect for up to a week as long as you are not dehydrated to begin with. So as soon as you are cast away in your rubber boat, start quaffing the brine. It takes a week to get your fishing organised, but this is phase two of Bombard's survival technique – fish juice. Though it sounds about as appetising as drinking dental mouthwash after a major cavity filling, fish juice will keep you alive. Make incisions along the length of the fish just below the dorsal fin and also along the underside. Then squeeze the juice out of the thing (having first gutted it.) A better way is to cube up the flesh and put it into a lemon squeezer – 2–3kg of fish flesh produces a litre of water. Don't forget the eyeballs, which are full of moisture.

In a mean air temperature of 32°C you can go three days without water. At 21°C you can go eight days; at 15°C a whopping seventeen days without a drink. With judicious mixing of seawater, fish juice and rain you too can survive. Further re-hydration can be achieved by giving yourself regular saltwater enemas using the raft pump and tube, though this procedure is not universally esteemed.

Food at sea is fish and fishing is about patience. Fish tend to follow rubber rafts after the first few days as seaweed and barnacles begin to attach themselves to the boat. Watch your

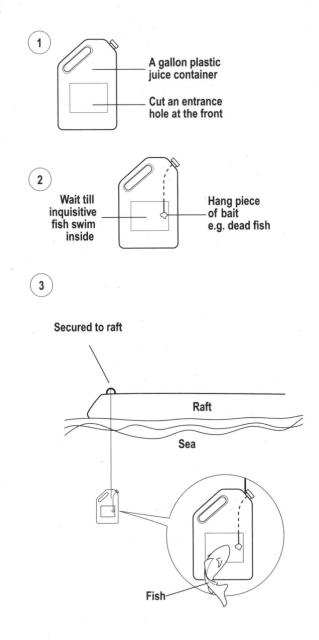

1

A gallon plastic juice container

Cut an entrance hole at the front

2

Wait till inquisitive fish swim inside

Hang piece of bait e.g. dead fish

3

Secured to raft

Raft

Sea

Fish

prey and use a gaff to catch them. The gaff is simply a hook on a pole – you can bind a bent piece of cutlery or a nail to a broom handle or oar to make one. Slowly dip the gaff in the water and though it may scare the fish at first, they will soon return. At the right moment impale the creature or even just flip it into the boat.

A rather nifty trap can be fashioned by cutting the face out of a gallon plastic juice container and hanging some bait in it (see diagram). You lower this into the water and wait for greedy triggerfish to swim in and investigate. You then scoop the whole thing out of the water and into the raft. Most successful castaways eventually get good at flipping fish and turtles into their rafts with their bare hands, a skill that could be practised while tickling trout (see trout tickling entry, page 82).

Your main enemy is, of course, inside you. The wreck of the *Medusa* is taken as an example of how wrong things can go if you lose your head. Cannibalism had broken out by the third day, even though humans can go three weeks without food and survive. After thirteen days thirteen people were left on the cannibal raft: 133 had perished.

---

15 Become a master of disguise

There are times in every man's life when a little disguise is called for, even if it is just to beat the snooping of neighbours or the local press, should you perchance become an object of interest to the media. More seriously, facial recognition technology can result in a serious misapplication of justice, should you be picked up through accidental confusion with a known felon or a suspected international terror merchant. The fact is, as all police forces know, facial recognition through video footage is far from perfect. Your best bet is to emulate 'the General', the renegade Irish crook, who went everywhere in public with his hand hiding his jaw, though this could become tedious and might mark you out as being a tad eccentric on the morning commute to work.

There is always the old standby of balaclava and dark glasses, but these days, unless skiing, they look as fishy as hell. That leaves false beards, flat caps, neck scarves and ear mufflers. Actually, a deer stalker is a good disguise when it comes to facial recognition software as it hides both the ears and the eyes. As a general rule, if you wear dark glasses, iPod earphones to cover your ears and a hat of some sort, then most software will not pick you up.

Then there are the more humorous possibilities of real disguise. Baden Powell, founder of the Boy Scout movement, whose macabre hobby was collecting instruments of death such as old guillotines and hangman's nooses, was very fond of disguise. The main point he made was to change one's skin colour, one's silhouette and one's habitual clothing. Skin should be lightened or darkened accordingly, in some cases using flour or shoe polish, but this, the Boy Scout founder points out, is only for emergencies. Changing your aspect or shape is possible by becoming fatter (pillows up the jumper) and older, perhaps with the addition of a walking stick or crutch or even a wheelchair. To change your clothing simply dress in a style you consider in unspeakably bad taste. Even your worst enemies won't recognise you.

---

16 The Achilles heel of modern life

Knees. It's chairs and cars that have done us in, so to avoid getting knee problems your first best bet is to sit as much as you can on the floor and to walk rather than drive. Basketball players who play guard position get far fewer knee injuries than other players – the reason being the amount of time they spend running backwards. Running backwards builds little-used knee muscles that help keep the whole assembly in place. Largely that's what a knee injury starts as – a slackening of muscles through under use and then sudden exertion; cartilage or bone slips and then you have an injury that can just keep on getting worse.

The best protection against long-term injury is plenty of regular walking over rough and uneven terrain. Forget jogging on tarmac: stride over boulder fields and pebbly beaches. The side shocks will help build all-round muscle strength. But don't binge on this after years of inactivity; build up slowly and practise regularly. Investigate the knee health of yoga practitioners.

Cycling is very good as a way of keeping the knee fit without shocking it too much. The constant low-level exercise maintains the muscles' tautness. Run up all flights of stairs, never take elevators if you can avoid them and kneel for five minutes before the TV news or a favourite programme; tell sceptical friends you are worshipping your favourite celebrity.

Minor knee injuries respond to love and attention. Massage the hurt or swollen knee each night before bed. Use hot towels on protesting knees before the massage to reduce pain, or ice if the injury has only just occurred. Deep heat can be rubbed in, too. The cure is mainly in directing the body's attention to the hurt spot so that self-healing can occur. The worst thing is to ignore it and hope that it will go away.

Finally, if you do suffer a major injury do not always opt immediately for surgery. Instead find the best physiotherapist you can who works with athletes, soccer and particularly rugby players and see if building different muscle groups and tendons through specific exercise might work as well.

17 How to make a potato gun

There are plans for such devices on the Internet, but some are less reliable than others. The below should give you an overview of what to look for.

But first, a potato gun is not a toy! Oh no, like Jonesy in *Dad's Army* with his weed-killer rocket you will be the proud owner of a lethal bit of artillery. Woe betide anyone foolish enough to be in range when you start lobbing those King Edwards about.

You will need: a three- to five-foot length of plastic drainpipe, UHU plastic glue, a drainpipe 'end' seal, a drill, plastic putty, an electric spark lighter for a cooker, WD40 or aerosol hairspray, a file and a bucket of big baked potato-sized spuds.

Chamfer the end of the drainpipe with the file so that it cuts a bit into the spud when you ram it down – this makes a tight seal. At the other end attach with glue the pipe 'end' seal – you can buy these from any DIY superstore. Drill a hole above this just wide enough to fit the head of the sparker into the tube side. Seal it in with plastic putty from a joke shop. Twist several big wide rubber bands around the pipe and fasten the contraption to your car roofrack (should you wish to attack other vehicles) or, more sensibly, a fence post or some other sturdy upright. Spray WD40 down the barrel, jam home a spud and then click the spark lighter. The potato should go at least 100m in a high curving trajectory.

18 Breaking into a car and hotwiring it

THIS IS HARD ON MODERN CARS. But it's quite easy on Land Rovers and any other older models you see out on the street. I'm assuming, of course, that the car in question is needed for a life-threatening emergency and not just a joyride into the nearest ornamental pond.

First you have to get inside. With cars that still have the pop up security locks on the door top, slide a piece of packing tape (the thin stiff nylon stuff around big heavy parcels) through the door gap and around the lock head. Then pop it up. You can also try a coat hanger, but this isn't easy and maybe you're in a hurry to get to the hospital or some other important place.

Use a rock. Smash out the side window making sure you don't cut your fingers in the process. Once inside you have to break the steering lock (if it's a really old car there won't be one) and then hotwire the ignition. Remove, with a chisel and hammer or screwdriver and hammer, all the plastic around the steering wheel underside. Pull off the steering wheel cover and undo the nut of the wheel – in other words, take it off. This reveals the lock and the ignition key barrel (you don't have to take the steering wheel off, but it's easier). Drive the chisel into the part where a nub of metal connects behind the key barrel to lock the wheel. Keep smashing like crazy and you will eventually break the key barrel out of its cylinder. Once this is removed you can release the lock. Then place a screwdriver into the empty barrel case and turn – this will start the car. Drive away – having first replaced the steering wheel.

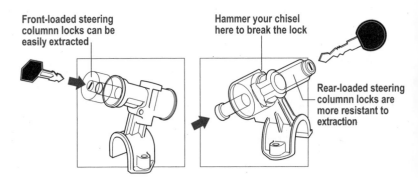

Front-loaded steering columnn locks can be easily extracted

Hammer your chisel here to break the lock

Rear-loaded steering columnn locks are more resistant to extraction

If this sounds long and messy, it is (in movie terms, in any case), but it took me about ten minutes in real life. If you smash with enough aggression, with the steering wheel still on, you can probably break the lock without removing the key barrel. Alternatively, you can thread a short crowbar through the steering wheel, jerk it hard to the left and right and, using this leverage internally, smash the steering lock. Then pull all the wires down from the ignition (there are always at least four) and see where their connectors are. Using a short piece of wire, experiment with shorting across two connectors. This should also start the engine.

If you really need to get into a modern car, just break the window or drill with a metal drill next to the boot lock. Reach in with a bent wire to pop the boot lock release wire. On some cars you can worm your way in from the boot without setting the alarm off. You then pop the bonnet and disconnect the battery, break the steering lock, reconnect the battery when you are ready, hotwire it and off you go.

19 Run with the bulls

Thanks to Ernest Hemingway, running the bulls in Pamplona has become something of a must for any young man seeking to prove he has *cojones* the size of cricket balls. Despite the odd fatality each year or two (there have been fifteen deaths since 1924, the last in 1995 – an American tourist) it is in fact quite a safe, though intensely invigorating, endeavour. It is also immensely crowded and you are more likely to be injured by the crowd pushing you into some obstacle than by being trampled and gored by an enraged bull.

You turn up, if keen, dressed in the red and white of the traditional bull runner. The course is a mere 800m in Pamplona (though there are other longer and shorter bull runs in other towns all over Spain); it is a straight sprint to the bullring at the other side of town. You make sure you have a rolled-up newspaper to whack the bull on the head if things get too risky. The side-streets are all blocked off with metal and wooden barricades, but with a small enough gap for a runner to sneak behind if he feels threatened by a bull. A rocket is fired which signals the release of the six bulls. I know, only six – the image you may have is of far more. Actually a second wave of cattle is later released, steers, much younger cattle, sent through to pick up any bulls that have given up running and are stuck in the streets being pestered by small boys lobbing fruit and newspapers at them.

You leg it like crazy in front of the bulls and in a good year they will pass you en masse. Otherwise you duck and dive your way from barrier to barrier until you enter the ring like a conquering hero. The secret of bulls is that they are herd animals. In a group they are harmless; separated out, one on one, they can be rather nasty. Even two bulls would much rather play at following each other than mess with some tourist holding a soggy paper and trying to look like papa Hemingway.

Remember, all along the route there are escape routes you can dodge through and the bull can't follow. The idea is to get into the ring or as close to the ring before ducking out. At the ring more hardy locals leap in and out further tormenting the poor old bulls.

If bull running isn't hard enough for you, you might consider facing a charging cow armed with a sword and cape. If you want to face a charging bull then you will have to kill it, by law, as a bull learns in the fifteen minutes before it is killed enough to be deadly to the next human being it meets. All the bulls at Pamplona and other fights have been running free for two to four years on the Spanish range with very little contact at all with human beings. Why else would they fall for that simple red cape trick?

Cows, however, are exempt from the legal requirement to be killed, which is why they are used for practice. However, even cows can be deadly. English matador Franc Evans was gored so deeply in the rectum by a cow in Salamanca that it punctured his bladder and only a swift police escort to the hospital saved his life.

You enter the ring holding the cape in one hand sticking out using the sword to extend it. For some reason most capes are pink not red, but they still cause the animal to charge. Stand your ground sideways on. Trust the cape. This is the crux of it. Even a wily cow will head for the middle of the biggest target – and that is the cape. As the cow approaches, execute a *suerte*, a pass, by sweeping the cape over the back of the moving cow and stepping forward. Then turn and meet the next charge and so on until you've had enough. Then run to hide behind the wooden *barrera*. A bull or cow takes a while to turn, and this is your chance to get in position for the next charge. Olé!

---

20 Face a charging bear

Bears in national parks, both in Canada and the USA, can be accustomed to tourists, feast on garbage and otherwise look real friendly. But be warned, a bear is a wild animal, and all wild animals are unpredictable. As one old trapper put it, 'Bears can seem predictable, but really that's just them being unpredictable in their unpredictability.'

Take comfort, though, from the world expert on bear attacks, Stephen Herrero, who states there has never been an attack on any group of five or more people. Other cool bits of information to mull over as you lope through the wilderness taut with anxiety include knowing: no bear has ever climbed higher up a tree than 33ft; grizzly bears rarely climb trees; most black bear charges are a try-on and if you make enough noise almost all bears will run away.

In North America, there are black bears (which can sometimes be brown in colour) and grizzly bears. In Europe our bears are so endangered and timid they pose no risk at all. Grizzlies occur in Siberia and are just as potentially dangerous as their American cousins. For most purposes then it is either black bears or the slightly larger grizzly bear that one should be wary of.

Current wisdom as widely disseminated by park rangers is broadly that if a black bear attacks fight back, but if a grizzly attacks play dead. That's right, if a grizzly bear is gnawing on your scalp and is already down to the bone, bite your tongue and pretend you aren't alive. This is a distillation of many, many attacks, but is so general as to be largely useless. Far more important is knowing how to minimise the chances of such an attack happening in the first place.

Bears of any kind hate being surprised. They hate it even more if they are surprised when they are with cubs or near to their cubs. So one should avoid surprising bears. Blundering along trails at twilight, jogging alone without a warning bell jingling from your backpack – these are ways you can stumble inadvertently upon a bear. If you catch sight of a bear, any kind, make a noise to scare them away. Shouting, banging pots together, firing off an aerosol yachting horn, blowing a loud whistle – all these have scared bears away, though they are not 100 per cent foolproof. If a group of bears are eating in your vicinity, making a noise won't always get them to stay away; even if they scarper to start with, plain curiosity will bring them back. But speaking from my own experience of being charged by a black bear: hold your ground. I had only a charred stick in my hands hastily snatched from a fire and a fading yacht air horn. The bear kept coming until it was a few yards away – then it turned tail and ran.

Grizzlies are different. If they don't mosey on away (they don't sprint fearfully like black bears do) after you have made a noise then keep making a noise while watching what they do. If a grizzly stands up on its hind legs and starts clicking its teeth and then begins to circle slowly, then you better find a good tree to climb – he means business.

Hungry bears are dangerous bears. If you are moving camp every day you don't need to worry too much about being sniffed out by a bear. They are cautious – up to a point – and you only need to be on your guard all the time if you stick around. Don't bother hauling food into trees – it takes for ever – simply use sealable waterproof cases or bags to store any odorous food and keep all food and the camp kitchen a good 100m from your tents. From numerous experiences I have found bears coming to investigate a camp just after sunrise – but never before. So get up early and be ready.

Dogs, especially big dogs – huskies and cattle dogs – generally keep bears away.

If you decide to go armed into the bush make sure you can handle the gun and keep it near and loaded – there have been cases of armed parties being mauled as they try to find their guns.

If a grizzly charges I would be tempted to throw something. A couple from the UK had their baby daughter picked up by a grizzly. The mother didn't play dead – she started hitting the thing with her shoe. The baby was dropped and the bear escaped.

Bears that want food, or are injured, or have grown used to human cooked food, can be troublesome. If a bear surprises you while eating, don't run with the food. Set it down for the bear to eat.

Bear spray is a kind of large size anti-mugger pepper spray. If you used it on a mugger he'd be down for days. On a grizzly it has worked, but you need to be close. Bear bangers are like thunder-flashes – they make a big noise and should scare away most bears. You can get both in any camping store in North America, but not in the UK.

Solo hiker Chris Townsend walked the entire length of the Canadian Rockies through serious grizzly country and had no problems at all. He used a whistle and made a noise whenever he saw bears and not once was he charged.

21 Deal with a shark attack

Sharks are like the undersea equivalent of bears – everyone wants to see them, but everyone is scared of being eaten alive, or even eaten dead. We've all seen *Jaws*. Anyone who has dived has received lots of assurances that sharks are mainly harmless, but that doesn't reassure many. Deep down we know those sharks are all killers.

Killers maybe, but also cowards. Sharks usually bump before they bite. They don't like getting hurt – even a little bit – in the pursuit of prey. Sharks have barely evolved in sixty-five million years, so they must be doing something right. The main thing is their fight strategy. A cowardly strategy means a longer life as long as you can fight back when you have to. There are more dead soldiers with VCs than living ones. Bravery tends to get bred out over time. Any brave sharks long ago got eaten by dolphins (their main predator surprisingly), so by triggering their coward switch you will probably survive.

People who swim with sharks, both in and out of shark cages, have one piece of essential equipment – a broom handle with a nail either through the end or taped to the end. This pointed prong is all you need to remind sharks that you are a little dangerous yourself. A shark is not a human. If you prod him on the hooter, he doesn't plot 'revenge', he calculates that he'd better give you a wide berth if he wants to remain alive.

As I mentioned, before they bite they bump. This is the signal you need to know that the sharks are hungry and potentially dangerous. Most sharks will just swim on by, especially if they aren't hungry. But if they circle and bump, you hit back with something sharp – a dive knife, an underwater spear or best of all your nail-spiked broom handle.

As for splashing or not splashing, there is little to choose from the two. Splashing is supposed to make the shark think you are a fish in trouble. But sharks don't think. If a shark is hungry it will investigate both splashers and non-splashers and in that case you should give the creature a good spike on the snout. In the true story on which the film *Open Water* is based, a couple stranded out at sea in diving gear are reluctant to swim strongly towards land for fear that their splashing will attract sharks. This misinformation cost them their lives.

22 Take a Japanese bath

If in Tokyo, take a bath. The Japanese have public baths on most blocks in the city and even the suburbs. The outside of the bathhouse usually identifies itself with some tiny little Zen-type garden and a wooden door with carving or writing on it – something a little aesthetic even in a poor neighbourhood.

You go through and pay – not much; the great thing about Japan is that necessities – baths, the subway, white shirts ironed for you, sushi, whiskey – are not really so very expensive. I knew a bankrupt man once who lived on gyoza (a kind of dumpling) and whiskey and water from the tap. Anyway, this talk of booze is not misplaced, because the baths are a great place to sweat off a hangover, should you need to.

So you pay and then you get a plastic basket and a tiny

white towel which is actually also a washcloth or flannel and you're in. You first enter a place where you can get changed, then, stark naked or with the tiny towel stretched around your waist, you make your way to the massive taps which have plastic bowls scattered around them. Since no soap is supposed to get into the main bath, this is where you actually do the washing; a general soaking and a light cleaning of the more objectionable parts of the body before gingerly lowering yourself into the main bath. Often there are two: hot and super-hot. But there is also a cold tap at one end and you can sit under that to make a transition from cool to hot. The taps, both hot and cold, run to keep the bath at the right temperature all over. Then you scamper out and thoroughly scrub yourself all over with the washcloth. Rinse it out in cold water and then put it on your head as you climb into the super-hot bath. Strangely, you will be able to stand the heat now and the towel will serve to cool your head down.

After a meditative time keeping your eyes averted in a modest way, you rise, drained and pleasantly exhausted, to enjoy a cold shower before towelling yourself off with the wrung-out washcloth. Then it's time for a hot sake or a cold Sapporo beer.

---

23 How to tell the sex of an earwig

This is a pretty good one for barbecues where you may be called upon to impress people with your backwoods knowledge and savoir faire. Or, perhaps, while sleeping under the stars with your special friend or loved one an earwig might chance upon her pillow causing an unpleasant incident defused only by asking: now was it a male or a female earwig?

The way to tell is simple and conclusive. The male earwig has curved, almost semi-circular, pincers that have a gap between them. The female has straight pincers that nearly touch.

24 Deal with a bee swarm

Bees usually swarm in spring or early summer. You may wish to take advantage of bees swarming in your garden to start your own beehive. Many beekeepers start just this way. The bees have swarmed with their queen to find new pastures. They will be placid from having gorged on honey to charge themselves up for the move. *Fairly* placid. Typically they will be hanging in a great buzzing ball from a bough in your garden and scaring the neighbours who will all have watched *Revenge of the Killer Bees* and right now are sheltering their little ones behind locked and bolted French windows. Rather than reach for the phone number for Rentakil or pest control, why not capture the bees yourself? If you have a history of anaphylactic shock reactions to bee stings this may not be a good idea, but if not, read on.

You will find a boiler suit quite handy as there is no gap at the waist for the bees to swarm down. Or up. Also, smooth fabrics are better than woolly, felt-like ones. Avoid suede (fairly unlikely that you would don suede trousers to go on a bee mission, but you've been warned) as this riles bees and causes them to sting, whereas they tend to leave smooth surfaces alone. You could wear gloves, but many beekeepers don't. Make sure you emit a bee-friendly vibe rather than a paranoid one. Remember a bee dies (the sting tears out a chunk of its abdomen) when it stings you, so they really don't want to sting you. If you do get stung remember that beekeepers never get arthritis, something in the venom counteracts the auto-immune reaction of arthritis. This knowledge will make you feel better. Wear a non-woolly hat. Tuck trousers into wellies.

Further pacification of bees is usually managed with a handy little smoker. You can improvise by building a small leafy bonfire under the swarm. Next you must either cut the branch off or knock the swarm into some kind of receptacle like a large box with a lid, a tea chest, the box your TV came in or even a sack. If you go for the cutting option the best saw is one of those super-sharp trimming saws attached to a long pole. Otherwise you're up in that tree yourself. Position your receptacle beneath the swarm to catch it. Get it as close as you can. To detach the swarm get a long hollow pole, like the kind that support TV aerials, and thread a length of coaxial cable or wire through it into a loop poking out at one end. Raise this over the swarm and gently tighten by pulling the wires tight at the bottom. The closing noose will sever the swarm and they will drop into the box if it is close enough. Shaking and joggling both will help.

Once you have your bees in a box you need a hive. Seed the hive with some combs of honey taken from those organic jars of comb honey. Upend the box, again having first held it over the smoker or smoking fire. The bees will quickly adapt to their new home.

If bees swarm your head and you're fit, start running; they'll follow, but not for ever. There have been several cases of people dying of heart attacks caused not by stings but by running from bees in hot weather while clad in beekeeping gear. If you have a fire extinguisher, especially a foam one, fire it with adequate caution at your head. Shaving foam and foam whipping cream work, too – it makes a no-fly zone around your head. You then swipe the bees off and put on a hat and scarf or other total head cover. Hosing them with water is another favourite, as is diving under water – though they will wait for you to surface, so have some kind of head covering ready.

---

25 Fancy driving tricks in sand, snow and mud

Most people come unstuck in sand, or rather stuck. When you start to get bogged down the natural reaction is to rev up. This just digs you in. Instead throttle back and creep out. As long as you are moving forward, even incrementally, you will escape. If you cease moving, stop immediately and get someone to push.

But getting stuck in sand in the first place usually happens through driving too slowly across the stuff. At low speeds sand is sticky, but as you pass the magic 30mph barrier it starts to fly by with you skimming its surface. If you can let your tyres down to half their normal pressure, do. It works wonders. You can let tyres down to 10psi and if you drive carefully it will be fine.

When driving up sand dunes it's best to get up lots of momentum. Driving down put the car in first gear and simply coast in a straight line. Don't go at an angle to the slope or you'll roll. If you start to slide sideways accelerate to correct rather than brake, which will exacerbate the slide.

Snow is slippery but sand isn't. Snow compacts under pressure, sand doesn't. Both respond to lower tyre pressure. You benefit from deep treads in snow, but they aren't needed in sand. Wheel spinning in snow may dig you down to a layer where you can get a grip, but this doesn't happen in sand.

Wheel spinning in mud can clear the treads, so it isn't such a bad thing to do as it is in sand.

When traversing water without a waterproofed engine and snorkel tube you need to remember two things: constant but low speed and reasonably high revs to keep the exhaust clear. You want to stop a big splashy wave dousing the electrical parts and you want to avoid a float. If you get the slightest sensation of drifting and you know or suspect deeper water ahead then brace yourself for a ride. Sometimes the spinning wheels act like propellers and get you across the bad stuff – more usually, though, you end up stuck in a tree downstream. You could try reversing, but usually water floods the exhaust pipe unless the revs are kept high.

If you drive too slowly through water at too low revs you will stall – and then it will be very hard to start again. But too fast can be equally disastrous. Mud, snow and sand can be crossed at high speed as long as there is no turning to be done. Avoid braking to a halt in these conditions as you will dig in. It's better to coast to a halt with the clutch disengaged.

If you drive through mud start your wipers before the crossing, otherwise the build-up of muck on the screen may stop them from working.

26 Dolphin riding for the curious

Dolphins eat sharks. Dolphins can be nasty. Susan Sarandon was once attacked by a jealous female dolphin while she was playing and 'riding' her mate. I suppose any attractive movie star fooling with a married man is asking for trouble from the jealous wife. Sarandon got a warning nip on the wrist that took months to heal. A real bite would have been fatal.

So when you go looking for dolphins to ride make sure they're single. Bottlenose dolphins are best. Dolphins, and whales, are born underwater and have to struggle to the surface to get their first breath. Adults lift the young up to the surface on their backs. We may surmise that the instinct to give rides to humans is connected with this.

To get a ride you just hang on to the dorsal fin and drape yourself alongside the dolphin. But take a deep breath first as you'll be underwater some of the time. You can also get a push with the dolphin using its snout against the soles of your feet. Sitting astride a dolphin can be viewed as insulting to some dolphinophiles.

27 Bodybuilding for the wary and short of time

No body is perfect. Start building yours today. Take a leaf out of the book of nutty Japanese writer Yukio Mishima who went from an emaciated starveling weighing 55kg to a strapping star of Yakuza films. Just don't take it too far and commit hara-kiri when you don't win the Nobel Prize.

Weight training began with 'dumb' bells, literally, as eighteenth-century essayist Joseph Addison observed that bell ringers had good physiques and arranged for a rope and a 'dumb bell' to be installed in his Oxford rooms. The other antecedent of modern weight training is the plethora of machines constructed for the rehabilitation of the hideously wounded after the First World War. From these odd beginnings we fast-forward to the slick chrome and Lycra-infested sweat factory of the modern gym.

But going to a gym, though pleasant at first, is, unless you have a good pal to go with and encourage you, a tedious chore after a relatively short time. Not only must you find a training chum, you must find one who wants to train when you want to train and who lives in the same area and pretty soon it all becomes complicated and so one ends up training alone … and giving up.

The solution is simple: build the gym in your own home! To join even a half-decent gym costs £600 to £1,000 a year. Instead of spending all that money buy your own equipment – from the small ads or from car boot sales – for a fraction of the cost. People are always buying weights, running machines, cycles and giving up and then selling them for a pittance, pretending they are well used, as if ashamed to ask the true price as that would reveal they had actually never used the said apparatus more than once. You can tap into this guilt by offering minimal money for expensive gear. Even if they refuse, there is always someone else who will part with a full set of weights for £25.

At this point you may be asking – hold on, if everyone else gives up as soon as they get all the gear, why should I be any different? For two reasons: quantity of gear and a sly and cunning methodology. Would-be fitness freaks usually buy one or two pieces of gear. They do not build an entire gym. This is the first mistake: one machine only is boring. You need a running machine, a decent cycle, a full set of weights, a bench press set-up, several chin-bars, hand dumb bells, a heavy punch bag, mirrors and a combination weights machine for pushing and pulling when free weights don't appeal. Second hand you can get the lot for under £300 – half your yearly membership. The next part is really clever: park the bike and the running machine in front of the television. Have a stack of must-watch DVDs or a subscription to TV channels you love to watch. Riding for an hour is easy when you are absorbed in Tarkovsky's *Stalker* or even *Ferris Bueller's Day Off*. Install those expandable chin-bars (Argos, under a tenner) at the top of each door frame. Every time you walk into a room you charge yourself a chin-up 'toll'. For some rooms the toll includes bringing your legs up to a right angle, which is great for the stomach. On the bathroom chin-bar hang a heavy punch bag and give it a good pasting every time you need to visit the loo. Soon the dividends will begin to show.

All stairs must be taken at a run, lifts scorned and even tube escalators abjured for the lovely long staircases of the Central and Piccadilly lines. Without having to jog an inch or even submit to an embarrassing interview and blood pressure test at your local gym you're already on your way to a whole new body.

Time now to up the exertion. Start running when you watch the news – morning and night. Sling on a rucksack with up to 40kg of weights inside – that will build your calves nicely; the hardest muscle to expand. If you find music inspires you, play the theme from *Rocky* and *Chariots of Fire* endlessly as you clink and groan with armfuls of shouldered metal. Early Massive Attack is good for sit-ups.

Flabby muscle tones up in two weeks so, if once you were buff, again it shall be so. To build muscle significantly takes longer – about three months. To build the tendons and skeletal support for handling heavier weights takes longer the older you are. Some idea can be got from the time a tendon injury takes to heal – often up to a year. Joints and tendons are the parts you need to be careful of, especially after a lay-off that follows a period of intense training, as that is when most joint damage occurs.

If long telephone calls need to be made, do it using a head set as you pound the treadmill or, if that sounds too out of breath, as you gently peddle or lift weights without straining.

Stretching exercises, good for the beginning and end of any workout, can also be done while on the phone. If you are canny with computers one can cycle on a bike with a laptop lightly grasped allowing for emails to be sent and read while the lower regions do the legwork. One can easily devise a truncated form of yoga where all the positions are tackled while operating your BlackBerry. *In all seriousness.*

Even with your own gym some days you'll feel lazy. If you can't make that mental leap into actually exercising, make yourself a hot chocolate and just saunter into your gym area. With a drink in hand you can start exercising without really having to decide to exercise. When friends come round force them into embarrassing shows of strength, which is again a covert way of getting your workout.

Pretty soon, as if by magic, you'll be kicking metaphorical sand in the world's face.

28 Survive a knife attack in San Quentin prison

Due to some hideous clerical error at immigration, your trip to California to visit Disneyworld and Universal studios has ended up with you being banged up in one of the world's nastiest prisons. Or so we are led to believe from the *Shawshank Redemption* and other such movies that seem to imply that every middle-class butt is like a rose-scented Brazilian supermodel to the leering ranks of sex-starved hardened cons in every jail. Forget it. Read Howard Marks' autobiography for the reality of US prison life – extreme tedium with a negotiable violence factor as long as you don't want to be part of the jailhouse mafia who run things.

However, what happens if your number is up and someone wants you 'shanked', i.e., stuck with a sliver of Perspex or a piece of sharpened cutlery nicked from the warder's canteen?

Obviously you need to ask for a transfer to some less-heated environment, but en route some precautions can be taken. Big, thick magazines and blockbuster novels can be used as body armour to protect the all important sides, stomach and lower back. A single unlucky stab around there can result in an internal bleed-out, leading to death in half an hour. Naturally you want to protect your heart, neck and lungs too, but these are less susceptible to sneaky attacks than the lower targets. If you are unlucky enough to be cornered in your cell then lie on your back up against the wall and kick like crazy, wounds to the legs may be nasty, but lower down seldom fatal. Yelling like crazy should bring the 'bulls' to your rescue.

Should you be forced into the unlikely situation of having to fight a knife duel with some deranged nutcase with no chance of parole then remember a few easy, er, pointers. Extend your left hand as a kind of shield and hold the knife back in your right hand sword style, not overhand dagger style. Accept you are going to get cut and maybe lose the use of a finger or two – but your aim is to survive. Do not focus on his knife or his eyes, but in the mid-area of his chest. That way you can see his moves coming. Ignore anything he says – just block it out. Remember that very few people actually have knife-fighting experience even if they have stabbed people to death. The knife is the sneaky coward's weapon of choice and people who get stabbed are usually unarmed. Circle and circle and keep away from getting backed up in a corner. If he holds his knife out front, like someone in a James Dean movie, cut his fingers off. If he still keeps on coming and no rescue is imminent, cut his arms some more and stab him repeatedly in the neck, chest, stomach etc (we are assuming this is a life and death situation here and your life is on the line).

If he holds back with a guarding left hand out front he knows how to fight, which is a bad sign. Keep shouting and circling and sacrificing the left hand and parrying with the right to gain time. Maybe you'll get lucky.

Next time you visit America make sure you don't crack any jokes with US immigration officials.

29 KGB technique for building fearlessness

Secret agents must be fearless and must be able to follow orders. One test employed when selecting agents was to seat them in a chair with arms, either a stacking plastic chair or more usually a hard-backed chair and ask them to rock back until they fell backwards.

Just think about it. All your childhood training has taught you it is dangerous, akin to suicide, to topple over backwards – at the very least you will crack your head open, if not break your neck.

Find an open space so there is nothing to hit as you fall backwards. Outside is fine, or in a gymnasium – which is where the Soviet Intelligence interviews took place – or simply a large room. Sit on the chair. Hold the sides and begin to topple – then fall. Instinctively you should bring your head forward rather than letting it fly backwards.

You're fine aren't you? The impact is taken across the whole of your back (don't use a chair with nasty knobbly turned sticks in its back-piece). Like a fakir who can tolerate a nailed bed by spreading the load, you too, when falling backwards, spread the load of the fall. As long as there is no object to bang your head on (a dresser or cooker behind you), you will be fine.

Go on – challenge your fear of falling and then challenge others.

---

30 Write a *haiku* poem

Haiku developed from the introductory *hokku* poem that would kick off a communal poetry writing session in medieval Japan known as *haikai*. In the late nineteenth century the *hokku* was lopped off and presented as a stand-alone poem known as *haiku*.

There are certain rules for writing *haiku*, more or less well known. What is under-appreciated in the West is that *haiku* is rooted in humour. Essentially it is a comic form. When Basho wrote (in the Allan Watts translation):

> *The old pond*
> *A frog jumps in:*
> *Plop!*

He wasn't trying to be heavy, he was trying to be comic, but not just comic, comic with a little extra, something to give pause for thought.

The main rules for traditional *haiku* poems are that they should be of seventeen syllables arranged 5–7–5 with a kind of cut in the middle formed by a set-up and an insight or summing up or Zen-like leap of mind. There should also be a 'season' word, which is simply a word that has an agreed link to the natural world in a particular season. In Basho's poem 'frog' is a spring season word.

Non-traditional *haiku* written in English can simply be

short poems around the seventeen-syllable mark.

Low on fuel
I see the Texaco sign
Tears of joy run down my face.

Haiku are a great way of capturing a moment with both pathos and comedy; for those requiring saltier fare, limericks may be preferred.

---

31 Ride that surfboard like Mark Foo

Mark Foo was a famous surfer who sought out big waves. He was unfortunately drowned and so became an iconic Bruce Lee-type figure. So maybe he's not the ideal role model, but you get the picture. In any case, it's always good if you can stand up on a surfboard rather than fall off it, repeatedly grazing your head and nose in the sand and getting walloped by the board on its bungee cord.

So take a one-day course. It's worth it. Failing that, the advice below will also work. If you have ridden snow or skateboards it's easier, but you still have to get the knack. It helps a lot if you actually like the water and have a wetsuit that is not constrictive and Dr's pro-plugs for your ears. Pro-plugs are used by freedivers as they let in water but slowly so your ears don't keep getting sluiced out – for repeated dunking they are great. You can buy them from music shops or from big dive stores.

Next get a user-friendly beginner's type medium board, nothing too fly and twitchy. Get a feel for it by riding it in on your stomach a few times. Get a feel for catching the waves; practise going further out and swimming the board to catch up with a wave. When you feel the board move with the wave jump up real quick.

This is the bit you need to practise repeatedly at home as it is very knackering if you do it again and again in the sea for the first time. Practise lying on the floor with your hands at about shoulder height and then jump up in one move. But jump up not with your feet facing forwards but sideways across the board (see diagram). If you stand crossways it's much easier to stay on. Practise that jump as one move. Many beginners try to kneel up, but that usually ends in disaster. Once up you will find it much easier to control than crouching down kneeling. And the movement from kneeling is an unstable one.

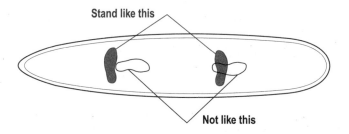

Stand like this

Not like this

Surfboards are a little forgiving. It's not like jumping up to stand on a unicycle saddle. By practising the one-jump, sideways stand you will very soon be riding those waves, maybe not like Mark Foo, but at least you'll feel like a seasoned pro.

32 Tricks with matches

You can have a lot of fun with a box of matches. Let's say you need to solder or otherwise fasten two bits of metal together in a sturdy manner. First shave off some slivers with a craft knife or a file from a silver coin – a 5p will do. Put the slivers in a spoon and then get five or six matches and strike them all at once and immediately hold them under the spoon – the metal will melt and can be used as solder. In the real-life escape from Alcatraz (upon which the Clint movie was based), the digging tool was made this way by brazing a spoon handle to the spike off a nail clipper.

The match/spoon trick was used by junkies in the past to liquefy heroin. The intense flare of three or more matches as they light is really very hot. At Christmas, if you pour neat cold brandy on a cool pudding it won't light. So if you are short of a way to get the Christmas pudding flaming (say you're in a restaurant), pour your brandy from the glass into the spoon, light three matches under it, get it so hot it self-ignites then pour it all over the pudding.

In Sweden, to return a borrowed matchbox with one head protruding is a homosexual recognition sign. Might be useful.

To split a match in two (in a desert island scenario), don't start at the wood end as you will always end up with a larger bit of head on one or even with shattering the head. Instead, insert the blade of your knife just below the head and gently apply pressure: the head will split and the shaft of the match will follow.

To light a match correctly first time so it doesn't break, support the head as well and when it lights move your fingers out of the way.

If you have to light a bonfire with a match and people are watching use two or even three together to avoid an embarrassing strike fest.

33 Play high stakes poker and win

Contrary to what you will hear, winning at high stakes poker is not about having the best hand, it's about winning chips. That doesn't mean you want bad hands, it means you must switch your focus from the cards to the chip pile. By skill, luck and guile you can maximise your good hands and minimise your bad hands to increase your chip pile.

Over time the luck of the draw evens out. Of course there are runs and sometimes you can really feel you are on a lucky streak, but over time it evens out. So the major characteristic you need is the discipline to stay for the long haul without getting bored. Poker is a strangely moral game as it teaches you to contain your greed and impatience. Even when you have schooled yourself to fold every hand you get that is not a winner you can still find yourself breaking your own rules and developing wishful thinking as the game progresses and your chip pile diminishes.

The most popular poker variant these days is Texas Hold'em. But whether playing this or any other kind the main tips for winning are similar.

1 Winning lots of small pots beats taking the odd big one. You are there to increase your chip pile not to wow people with the highest hand.

2 Identify the play and the players. Most beginners are loose. That means they are too hopeful about winning and don't

fold enough. Play tight to win – in other words, only play good hands.

3 Many players are weak – if you raise they run scared and start panicking – so if you identify that kind of player, you can bluff him by raising.

4 Some players are aggressive – they love to raise all the time. With these you stay in the game if it is cheap to do so and only play winning hands.

5 Loose players can be identified very often by their 'loose' stack of chips. Tight players indicate their anal retentiveness with a correspondingly neat pile. You'd be surprised how often this is true.

6 Weak players often keep peeking to check if they remembered their cards right. Often people forget what suits they have when they are under pressure, so a peek can indicate an intention to make a flush.

7 Many people do only two kinds of bluff – acting weak when strong and acting strong and loud when weak. Watch during the beginning rounds to see if this is the case.

8 Weak players often count and glance at the chips. Aggressive players seldom count their chips except to gloat. Both types can be beaten by playing an opposing style.

9 Aggressive players try to rile you, eyeball you or mouth off – this is all great as it means that you can keep them putting money into the game as they don't scare easy even when their hands are crap.

10 Bluffing can fail a lot and still make you money in the long run. Even if you lose a lot of bluffs, if your opponents fold even 10 per cent of the time you still end up winning more as long as twenty or more bets have been made.

34 How to win at croquet

There are very few occasions when a non-croquet player finds himself playing the game and fewer still when winning really counts. But for that once in a lifetime opportunity here are a few tips.

1 Croquet is a game where caution pays off. Incremental improving shots are better than going right past the hoop.

2 Identify the nice players who make mistakes. Capitalise on them and send their balls off the pitch.

3 Make a habit of croqueting every opponent before and after each hoop – i.e., miss no opportunity to croquet others.

4 Treat it like snooker not golf. Try to plan ahead how you will snooker others so they cannot get through the hoops.

5 If way behind, suggest a short drinks break and sneak back on to the pitch and move the balls. Also loosen your opponent's mallet heads so they mis-shoot.

35 Swim like Captain Webb

Captain Webb, breaststroker extraordinaire and the first man to swim the Channel, was always keen to convert weak swimmers into strong strokers through the application of a few basic principles.

The main one being: the purpose of moving the arms and legs is not to stay above the surface but to propel yourself forward. If you are keeping afloat through arm and leg strokes you will always tire easily and swim slowly. The object is to float in a hydrodynamic shape (as pointed and as flat as possible) and use the arms to keep you moving forward. It's that simple.

The first step in relearning how to swim is to float and stretch out and get used to that position in the water – that's your plimsoll line, so to speak. If your mouth is under water, get used to twisting it sideways to breathe if crawling, or when you break the surface when breasting. Wear goggles if chlorine annoys you. Dr's pro-plugs, mentioned earlier in connection to surfing, are well worth wearing to avoid ear infections.

Now start the stroke. The secret is in its prolongation and relaxed nature. For the crawl, the returning arm slaps or cuts the water with great ease not manic energy. The power only comes on – long and smooth – while the arm is underwater, swirling lengthways and longways as long underwater as it can, maximising the forward motion out of every stroke made. As soon as one is almost finished, before the pointed projectile of your body halts, the next arm has slipped in and is powering ahead. The legs? Just flip them up and down to keep time, keep them busy – they are of no importance in keeping up the power – they are just moved to ease the way forward and to prevent your body from flopping down and spoiling your hydrodynamics.

Breaststroke and butterfly can both benefit from the low in the water, relaxed and maximised stroke indicated above. The legs provide the lengthy relaxed stroke power here as well. Watch top swimmers and see how far they go on a single stroke – you can too as long as your body floats.

36 The last word on the perfect cup of tea

Tea is *the* drink, whatever the coffee addict might say. When too much coffee and the hectic meanderings of modern life reduce you to an insomniac or a man with the shakes there is always tea. Bearing in mind that a shift to drinking tea after twenty years of coffee takes a few days of mild headaches to accomplish and sometimes a general seizing up of the bowels, it will still amount to a sensational return! Good tea can be drunk all day long without giving you the shakes or turning your thoughts all paranoid and hyper; not for nothing does that old trooper Tony Benn carry around his tea mug and drink a gallon of the stuff a day and still be going strong at over eighty. Tea may not have the wallop of an espresso but it has staying power; it is a restorative after exertion or distress; it is quite simply the best drink going.

But how to make it? Even Twinings, who should know better, know very little about tea-making judging by the advice on their packets. Scientists from time to time make nonsensical statements such as 'the pot should not be heated' or 'boiling the leaves makes no difference'. Now, just as the waters of Burton-upon-Trent make excellent beer but those of London do not, so too the taste of tea depends on small subtleties of difference. The great scientist and traveller Francis Galton fixed a thermometer into his kettle in 1850 and, being also a connoisseur of tea and not a mere recorder of numbers, his findings tie in most closely with what I have found after a lifetime of steady tea tippling.

Unlike coffee and beer, tea is less affected by the hardness, or mineral quality, of the water – why I do not know. Perhaps that explains its great popularity in Britain. Henri Carpentier, the great French boxer, complained that even though he brought his coffee from France it never tasted right without French water and I am inclined to agree. Tea, on the other hand, travels much better.

The basic parameters, then, are not water quality but water temperature and brew time. Wrong quantities of either result in bitterness and flatness. Leave the leaves too long (or the bag, but that is most inferior) and you will get bitterness. Infuse in boiling or too hot water and bitterness again results. Use tepid water or leave too little time brewing and flatness of taste results.

Galton meticulously tried every combination of water temperature and length of brew time and arrived at this precise formula which I adhere to with astounding success: boil the water until it's bubbling, transfer to your teapot and warm the pot thoroughly. This pre-warming is essential to keep the temperature of the brew between 180–190°F. Those who deride pre-warming have inured themselves to the taste of flatness long ago. Bring the water back to the boil and, filling the teapot to the *two-thirds mark*, add to the leaves. Let them stand for four minutes and then add more freshly boiled water to fill the pot to the brim. This last refill of piping hot water keeps the brew above 180° for the crucial further four minutes – making a brew time of exactly eight minutes in all for a perfect cup.

As Galton puts it, 'The palate becomes far less fastidious about the quality of the second cup,' so further top-ups of the teapot do not seem to have a significant effect on the taste despite the long standing of the leaves.

Galton concludes: 'There is no other mystery in the teapot.'

Bedouin, of course, do none of the above and still manage to make a marvellous and revivifying brew. They add tea dust and leaves to a small tin teapot with an equal quantity of sugar and boil the whole thing in the embers of the fire. I think the key here is in boiling with the sugar, which takes out the bitterness at source, so to speak, leaving a drink of unusually refreshing qualities. It is drunk in glass shot glasses in several small hits.

37 Blisters afoot and the old Foreign Legion method

Not all hikers get blisters, but many do. It seems, too, that once a blister sufferer, always a blister sufferer. I have walked some very long distances and usually suffered blisters of one sort or another along the way. But at long last I have accumulated such a store of blister-busting knowledge that the suffering is, almost, a thing of the past.

Blisters are caused, in the main, by too tight boots or shoes. Shoes can raise bigger blisters than boots as the smaller surface area increases the pressure at any one point. This is an argument in favour of boots for the blister prone. Some folks can walk a thousand miles in old trainers and others need good-fitting leather boots.

The next consideration is size: boots that fit nicely for a day hike can kill you on a long distance walk. With a 15–20kg rucksack, your feet squash out a size and a half bigger than your usual shoe size. Forget buying boots with a snug fit. Wear plenty of socks and get bigger boots than your normal size. You may also consider getting double socks with a nylon liner, which some have found great at keeping blisters to a minimum.

Boots are best made of leather and the more supple the better. Oil them well with nikwax and, if new, crack a raw egg inside them before the maiden hike. If you want to get radical and copy German army practice, urinate on them.

Another blister-avoidance method that many swear by is to soap the inside of the sock, making a good lather while you are at it. But you're still probably going to get them. To minimise the discomfort, stop every hour and check for any redness. If an area seems to be getting rubbed, stick a moleskin plaster over that area. It's too late if a blister has already formed. For that you need the Foreign Legion method of popping blisters.

In the Foreign Legion they used to march long distances over sand. This is the worst terrain for blisters as the compacted sand compresses the boot around the foot and rubs it monotonously in the same spot. To keep marching the Legionaires pop their blisters as soon as they get them, but leave a piece of thread sewn through the blister with ends dangling. This drains fluid as you march on, for, as all blistered blusterers know, a popped blister seals up immediately and just keeps on growing. The threads can be removed when the blister has dried up.

At night, an application of salt held in place by a plaster can dry a blister out. In the morning you can cover it with moleskin and keep walking. An old and tested method for drying out blisters is to mix pure alcohol and candle wax in your palm and rub this into your feet at night. By morning the blisters will have departed.

Long acquaintance with the misery of blisters has led me to some inescapable conclusions. Water and damp aids their formation unless there is an excess of it, as in a wet-sock bootee. I walked hundreds of miles along rivers in wet-sock boots and never once got a blister. Merely sweaty feet blister quicker. Leather insoles absorb sweat best and open-toed sandals allow it to evaporate. For desert walking sandals are best as long as the straps don't rub (which you can guard against by sticking a moleskin plaster each morning on the areas where they touch the skin). I have seen people using Teva-type sandals and socks in the mountains and they all spoke highly of their comfort. If you change your socks often and switch socks around your feet blister less. Of course lots of training, including going around in bare feet, helps. Athletes' foot makes the feet very susceptible to blistering, so deal with that before a hike with cream, which is better by far than powder.

As long as you do something to alleviate your blisters they will slowly improve. Even silly little things like salting them or massaging your toes during a rest break helps. Unlike some maladies blisters *never* go away if you ignore them, they only get bigger.

38 Hope for those allergic to horseflies and other nasties

As a child I was bitten by a horsefly – a 'cleg' as they call them up north – and it caused my arm to swell to twice its normal size. Mosquitoes too can sometimes provoke an allergic reaction. I've even had bad bumps from ant bites. Thankfully it seems wasps and bees don't cause any problem except pain. The worst remains the horsefly.

Horseflies seem preternaturally stupid, hovering in a slow and ungainly way, relics of prehistory. Once they get their teeth in, filthy from cow or horse hide, they stay and suck and suck so they are easy to kill, but that's little recompense because your arm or leg or neck is already beginning to swell up.

I once walked a great distance in the Pyrenees through an area infested with horseflies. There were so many I didn't dare stop walking unless my legs were covered up first. I got so many bites my calves, thighs and the glands behind my knees were beginning to swell hugely and become painful, to the point where they interfered with walking. I thought I would have to give up. And then the final straw – a horsefly detached itself from the swarm, flew into my mouth and bit me on the tongue. After crunching it up and spitting it out I waited to die. If the swelling on my legs was anything to go by I could expect my tongue to double in size, block my throat and choke me.

Nothing happened. Saliva is an antidote to horsefly 'venom', the stuff they add to the mix to allow the blood to stop clotting and be sucked up into their hideous bodies. I then found by quick experiment that if I spat on my hand and rubbed saliva straight on to any bite as soon as it happened the bite never swelled up. Leave spitting on the bite more than thirty seconds, though, and it didn't work. But if you were quick the bite remained as a red mark only. By extension I found it worked for all biters, including deer flies, mosquitoes and gnats. This made me deliriously happy. No longer was I a victim of biting insects. No longer did I need to cower behind mosquito nets and tubes of repellent. Simple spit. I guarantee it works.

---

39 Picking locks the Nobel way

Nobel Prize-winner Richard Feynman was adept at picking locks. He was fascinated by the subject and was good at it. He even managed to crack several safes on the ultra-secure base where the A-Bomb was being developed. His technique for picking any Yale-type lock is easy to follow. It also works on most padlocks, indeed any lock where the turning moment can be transmitted by jamming a screwdriver into the front of the lock rather than in traditional locks where the unlocking power is provided by the projecting end of the key.

Tools: you can buy lock-picking kits and they work, but all the tools you need are easily to hand. A flathead screwdriver, a length of narrow stiff wire – this is the crucial bit – too soft and it will be useless, too wide and it won't work. Some very stiff hairpins work. A hatpin would be good. On some locks a bicycle spoke might be too wide, but that kind of strength is what we're looking for. Paperclips are useless as they are too easy to bend.

Jam the screwdriver into the lower part of the lock and apply a constant turning pressure. If someone else can do this it's actually a lot easier because you can then concentrate on the picking. Using the hairpin, which you need to bend up at the end to make a 'pick', you simply riffle back and forth along the tumblers that hang down from the top of the lock. As each tumbler is forced up the lock turns a fraction, jamming that tumbler in position. The reason it works is that the tumblers are never, however well the lock is made, all exactly in line. Some are further to one side than others. By riffling back and forth you discover which are bearing the brunt of the lock's turn at that point. When you poke it back the lock slips a fraction. Then you concentrate on the next one until all the tumblers have been forced back and the lock turns automatically.

Lock picking is always harder than it looks in the movies. Often one lock can take ten minutes. But it can be done and with practice and the right tools a whole new adventure with criminal overtones awaits you.

40 Light a fire with a coke can and a tube of toothpaste

Try this first as a warm-up. Suspend a ring inside a clear glass bottle from a piece of string held in place by a cork in the top. Challenge people to release the ring without touching the cork or the bottle. After much head scratching produce, on a sunny day, your magnifying glass and simply burn through the knot holding the ring.

Yep – back to fun with fire, and it's endless. The coke can trick is another great one for camping trips and barbecue bragfests. Get your can and make sure it has a nice smooth undamaged base. Squeeze on some toothpaste, best is the whitening kind as it has more abrasive. Start rubbing with your finger to produce a mirror shine. It may take a while, but it's worth it. Now use the resulting concave mirror to focus the sun's rays on a piece of tinder, dry cotton etc. Blow gently to cause fire.

If you fancy getting really fancy try carving a magnifying lens out of ice. To get ice without bubbles or imperfections isn't easy and defeats many people – but keep trying. The secret is in the slow freezing, which is why icicles are so clear. If you boil water for ten minutes most of the dissolved gases will have been driven out, but more will be reabsorbed as it cools, so use the water before it's cold. Fill a balloon with it and hang the balloon in your freezer. It will cool more slowly hanging than if it is lying on the inside of the freezer. You can also slow down the process by laying the balloon inside a bowl of water, which will tend to insulate it and slow the process down.

You can also get clear ice from lakes, but you may need to dig down through the top layer to get to the really clear stuff. In cold places break a hole in lake ice and the next morning collect the ice that has formed over the hole – it will always be clear.

As ice, and water, refracts light less powerfully than glass you will need a really fat, almost globular, lens. Cut away the balloon and shape the lens making it very curved on one side, hemispherical in fact, and slightly flatter on the other. Use a knife and wear gloves and do it in cold weather to reduce melting. Smooth the lens by hand melting with your gloves off, which is fairly painful.

If the ice is clear enough it should start a fire in seconds. Most failures are from ice that is too thin, lenses that are not curved enough and ice that is too frosty.

Fire from cling film and water is another good skill to have at your disposal and one that is far easier to accomplish than making fire from ice. Take a big piece of cling film, half a metre square. Line a small saucepan or Tupperware bowl with it and fill with water. Be careful not to puncture the film. Gather the edges together to seal the water in. Make a fist-sized film-wrapped bubble of water and manipulate the shape to make a magnifier. In the sun use it to focus rays on some tinder. It will soon begin to smoke and catch fire.

41 How to put a snake in a bag

This isn't easy to work out. You have your snake, maybe venomous, maybe not, but it's certainly capable of biting. You are holding the snake behind its head. It's not a big one, maybe a metre long. You have your bag. But if you poke the tail of the snake into the bag (which it will resist mightily), there will come a point when you will have to release the snake's head and quickly pull your hand out of the bag. In that nasty moment you may well get bitten.

The trick is as simple and as satisfying as cutting a Mobius strip in two and finding two linked circles. Turn your bag inside out and place it over your fist and the snake's head it is holding. Using your other hand close it over your fist through the bag. Delicately but firmly transfer the hold so that you are holding the snake's neck *through* the bag. Turn the bag the right way back up the snake's body. Now feed the rest of the snake through the grip you have and into the bag. As long as the bag is bite proof (bit silly if it isn't), the snake will be trapped inside with no danger to yourself.

An ancient Egyptian cure for snake fear was to have a viper or cobra bite a young boy on his earlobe. Though the pain is great there are insufficient blood vessels there for poisoning to occur.

Catching a snake requires speed and deliberation. A great help are nooses of rope which extend out of a tube, say a long bamboo. You pull at the other end and have the snake fast. Most snakes find snuff highly poisonous, so this can be used as a weapon of last resort. Running from snakes is a good idea as they have small hearts in comparison to their size. Though snakes can strike quickly they move more slowly – even the black mamba can be out-run by a fast human, and it will never follow for more than a few minutes before becoming exhausted. To capture a giant snake, exhaust it through restraining it with nooses and then imprison it in a big box or sack. Any snake longer than 22ft will find a caring home in one of the big American zoos. They will pay upwards of $20,000 for such a snake. Should you be feeling brave, you might try to claim the Roosevelt prize offered by the Bronx Zoo for any snake caught in excess of 30ft long. Started in 1912 the prize has yet to be claimed. My book *Big Snake* and the accompanying Channel 4 film go some way towards showing why it is still unclaimed, though our team did, in the end, manage to capture a reptile 26ft long.

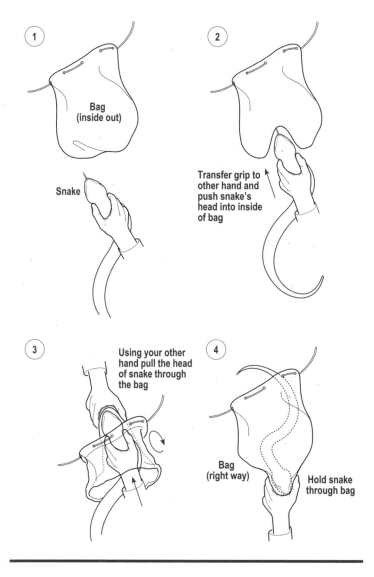

42 How to tickle trout

This is no joke I assure you. I have witnessed trout tickling in a stream in Derbyshire by a fourteen-year-old boy and eaten the trout he caught. It seemed like magic then, and it still does now. But it can be done and is easy, in fact, when you know how and, more importantly, where, the trout are hiding.

Trout tickling is a term that covers a gamut of hand-powered fishing techniques from scooping them out like a bear to sensuously stroking their underbellies into submission.

One way to practise the sensation of trout tickling and the kind of tactile skill you'll need is to search with two hands through a bubble bath for a bar of soap. Kind of gently play it between the hands until you can be sure to grab it. Then try it one handed.

Search for overhanging banks, in the downstream shadow of big rocks or, best of all, small streams with a small step of a waterfall, no more than a foot or so high. If you can see trout there, extend your hand very, very gently into the water – they'll scatter, but don't worry they'll be back to these rest places away from the stream's buffeting current. Start the tickling motion even if there is no trout to hand, and even if you have seen none (as long as it looks a likely place.) As your vision will probably be restricted by your lying or kneeling position you'll have to guess when you touch one. The main thing is to remember you want to touch and pet that fish – don't stiffen as if you've just brushed against a snake or it will flee. Trout like being tickled – it will stay as your fingers brush lightly against its underbelly. If you can, work your way up the fish's body so that you can grasp its head. Alternatively just flip it out onto the bank – but beware, flipped fish have a way of flipping themselves back in again.

Another method is to lie down with both hands in the water staring down into the under depths of a bank. If you wear Polaroid glasses you'll see better. Tickling with your fingers you may glimpse trout in the shadows. If a tail comes close or brushes against you bring the hands together and scoop it out.

Kill it with a stone, gut it, then ram a stick lengthways through it and cook on a small fire. What could be more satisfying or delicious?

---

43 Drive a T34 tank

Should you find yourself in a tricky situation in, say, the Central African Republic and suddenly require a few tank-driving skills, just how difficult is it?

There are still a few T34s in service in African and Middle Eastern countries – not bad going for a tank whose basic design is over seventy years old. The last European T34s fought in Bosnia and Croatia in the 1990s. One was recently recovered after having spent fifty-six years at the bottom of a muddy bog in Estonia and was quickly restored to full working condition.

Such longevity is a tribute to the brilliance of engineer M.I. Koshkin, who designed it in 1935. Every part of the T34 smacks of simplicity. It shouts it out from the crude welding on the hull to the barely filed-off cast imperfections of the turret. This is a war machine par excellence and, like the brilliant Kalashnikov rifle, is designed so that a moron can use it, repair it and, just as importantly, build it. The German tanks, though seductive in their own way, are inferior to the

Russian and American tanks because they are way too fancy; engineering dreams rather than crude objects that can be manufactured in their thousands. If the Second World War had any lesson it was: quantity always beats quality. As Stalin reputedly said, 'Quantity has a quality all of its own.'

Not that the T34 doesn't have other qualities – it does. The armour slopes like a much more modern tank, which means even a hit from an 88mm can be deflected. The tracks are as wide as a Chieftain – and were easily the widest during the Second World War – which means you sink less in mud and snow and go fast over rough ground. The suspension is modified Christie suspension 'borrowed' from the US but with guide wheels and drive wheels of the same large size, protecting to some extent the hull and making them easier to repair and unclog than smaller wheels. The engine is diesel – sheer genius – diesels don't 'brew up' when hit, like petrol-engined tanks – a major cause of death among Sherman drivers. Diesels run better if they are never switched off – great in an ice-bound country like Russia. Diesels also stink, so expect a headache if you drive for long. The T34 engine – twelve-cylinder, ultra-simple, 500bhp and capable of about a mile to the gallon – is situated in the hull without any kind of separation from the crew. Driving a T34 is like sitting under the bonnet of your car. Wear ear plugs. If you need to fill her up remember to have a wallet full of money – a T34 has a 545-litre tank.

Tanks, thankfully, are ultra basic, simpler, in a way, than cars to drive. Instead of steering and braking, the braking *is* the steering. Instead of a wheel you have two levers either side of your seat. Pull on the left lever and you turn left because you have braked the left set of tracks. Pull on the right brake lever and you turn right.

As driver of a T34 you shin up the side of the tank and

down through the turret, which is about ten feet off the ground. Wear a hat and long sleeves as there are an incredible number of sharp edges and levers to brain yourself on as you slide down into the metal driver's seat suspended between the two driving levers. The red button in front is the start button (no key needed) and the peddles at your feet are the clutch (no synchromesh) and the accelerator. On your right is the gear lever – very simple – with five forward gears and one reverse.

If it's a cold day, light a small fire under the engine – rags doused in diesel and set alight was a favourite trick on the Eastern Front. This will help the engine start and keep it from stalling, which is a special problem with big water-cooled diesels like the T34, until they've been running half an hour or more. With the engine (and the interior) now nice and warm, press the start button and gun the accelerator. It's impossible to blow up a T34 engine from over-revving, so rev it like crazy. Press the clutch twice or the gears won't engage, then shift it into first. Let out the clutch and you're moving. Squint through the narrow deep slot at the front or through the periscope, which is about as tiny and user-unfriendly as the viewfinder on a camera. You work through the gears quickly, like a truck driver – the T34 only has a top road speed of 32mph. When you head off road the engine's deafening protests will tell you when you need to change down to get more power. Again, because it's a diesel, the main power comes mid-range and not when you're screaming it, which is a sign to drop a gear.

Use the levers to make the turns, but don't expect it to be quick. Turning a tank is like turning a heavy sailing boat – allow several tank lengths to complete the move if you are running at any speed.

The main problem as driver is visibility. That's solved by

the commander up top bellowing instructions either through your earphones or down the hatch by shouting. But even if you hit a garden wall or two or even a carelessly parked car you'll find the 32-ton bulk of the T34 just keeps rolling along. If you get addicted you can buy your own fully restored one for about £15,000 – cheaper than a new Volvo and much safer in a collision.

44 Start your own political party and stand for Parliament

In the midst of annoyance at your local MP, or when faced by the sheer mediocrity of the line-up of candidates for a general election, think seriously of standing for Parliament yourself. It's a whole lot easier to bypass the silly shenanigans of 'getting selected' – either stand as an Independent, or, which is more fun, start your own political party.

This is easy and it doesn't have to be a very big party; you only need two members – the leader and someone willing to be treasurer, secretary etc. You need a logo, but make sure it isn't un-PC. When a new eco-party submitted the logo of a deer in the cross-hairs of a rifle sight (they were against the needless killing of animals), the logo was rejected as being 'possibly disturbing to some voters'.

Next, the cost: a mere £150, but you need to keep submitting quarterly statements to maintain your party's live status. These reports are simple to fill in as long as you have not received any donations. If you have, you must laboriously note them all down. All the information you need you can get from the Electoral Commission, who are very helpful and obviously keen on anyone other than the three or four main parties.

Now you have a party it's time to stand as an MP. This has gone up to £500, a sum you will lose if you poll less than 10 per cent of the votes – which you will, unless you're a celebrity like Martin Bell. But you can get a lot of mileage for your £500 – you get to go to all the hustings (political debates and meetings before the election), you get a free mail-out for up to 10,000 leaflets. But beware – folding 10,000 leaflets is a complete nightmare; you'll need all your loyal party members and your family, too.

To start the MP candidacy process you have to find six people in the constituency who don't think you're mad; harder than it sounds when you really start asking. Those six have to be registered on the electoral roll (though you don't, strangely). With their signatures on a paper which states they think you're a good potential candidate (tell waverers they don't actually *have* to vote for you, even though they have seconded your candidacy) you can pay your £500 deposit at the local council office and start campaigning.

This is when you discover the advantage of having a party machine behind you. To campaign alone is dispiriting. Turn up to hustings with friends bribed with drink. When it's your turn to answer questions show up the other candidates with your honesty and authenticity. They'll try to ignore you and belittle you, but bare your teeth – these are cowardly weaklings posturing to gain power for selfish ends, unlike yourself. Indeed you might make much of the paradox that the only person worth voting in is the one with no chance of getting in as he will be the only one with no motive for selling out.

Soldier on and use momentum to keep you going. Get on the radio and local TV by turning up to election publicity stunts organised by the main candidates. If you are wearing a distinctive costume – maybe a bottle-green blazer and slacks or a union jack jump suit – the press will look to you for light relief. Make the most of discomforting the major party candidates. Take inspiration from the fact that only a weasel would ever stand for one of these well-known parties with their incredible records of lying and dissimulation. Only you are clean!

On Election Day you and your 'agent' – which can be anyone – present yourselves at the poll counting station, which is usually a big school hall. Around midnight to 3 a.m. the count will come in. You and the other candidates will have a chance to look through the spoiled ballot papers and decide whether they really are spoiled. You may be surprised at how lacking in true vituperation and obscenity they are. The commonest 'spoil' is to scrawl 'none of the above'.

Then comes the announcement. The losers get announced first. After you've been pleasantly surprised by the fact that you got more than five votes, each candidate gets the chance to make a speech to the assembled crowd. Now's your chance, because this part is usually televised. Make a real stormer, but expect to be booed by the winner's party cohorts. Smile and congratulate the winner, but don't be surprised if they don't return this gentlemanly behaviour. The winner is already too busy planning how to get re-elected next time.

45 Escape from a POW camp

You've seen the *Great Escape* and the *Colditz Story* and perhaps the *Wooden Horse*, where three men used a vaulting horse as the cover for a tunnel dug near to the wire. But how would you fare if you suddenly found yourself banged up in a POW camp?

As F. Spencer Chapman, who stayed on the run behind Japanese lines for three years, always said – your best chance of escape is just after you've been captured. Unfortunately that's exactly when you feel least like escaping. Your morale is at rock bottom and you're beginning to believe all those arrogant Jerries who keep offering you a cigarette and saying: 'For you, Tommy, the war is over!'

The first opportunity, the first sign of laxity, leg it. Spencer Chapman was briefly caught by a Japanese patrol in Malaya. The first night of his capture he had to lie between enemy soldiers in a tent. By pretending to be sick and overheated by the nearby campfire he got the sentry to rake it further away, leaving his part of the tent in darkness. As the others slept he slyly loosened the tent pegs. Just before dawn he sprang up and bolted under the tent wall and into the jungle. With the element of surprise on his side, he remained free.

As soon as you get sent to a prisoner of war camp your chances of escaping are reduced. You will be far from your own lines and you'll be behind barbed wire. It will take time and determination to escape.

There are four choices: over the wire, under the wire, through the wire or through the front gate. Tunnelling under the wire takes time and materials. Over the wire is often overlooked. The fastest escape in the Second World War was the Warburg wire job – twenty-two men out in under two minutes, authored by the great Colditz engineer Jock Hamilton Baillie. Baillie constructed flip-top storming ladders which, once the camp electricity had been fused, were used to storm the inside wire, and then flip over to provide a bridge over the outside wire and then you dropped to the ground. Genius!

Through the wire with cutters is something guards are looking out for and is never as easy as it sounds. Through the front gate on your way to a hospital or a court martial might provide a chance to escape – perhaps by jumping from a train; jump backwards but face the direction the train's going and hit the ground running – but be prepared to roll and protect your head.

In the First World War the most successful escapes were walking escapes where the escaper trudged away by foot. By the Second World War the train-aided escape had become the most successful. With modern communications, surveillance and documentation, the quicker you are out of enemy territory the better.

In his successful escape from a Beirut kidnapping in 1987, journalist Charles Glass managed to use dark thread from his blindfold to tie the links of his chains together – thus shortening the chain. He managed to tie them together in

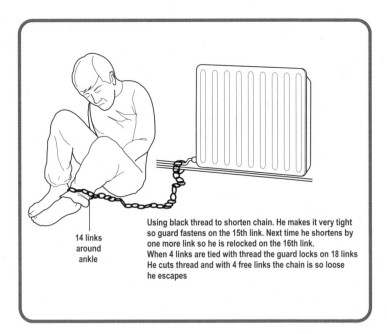

14 links around ankle

Using black thread to shorten chain. He makes it very tight so guard fastens on the 15th link. Next time he shortens by one more link so he is relocked on the 16th link.
When 4 links are tied with thread the guard locks on 18 links
He cuts thread and with 4 free links the chain is so loose he escapes

the few moments when the chain was removed. Once he was re-shackled the attached links concealed the chain's real length. The moment the guards were not looking he was able to snap the thread, lengthen the chain, release himself, sneak past the sleeping guard and get free.

The principles of escape remain unchanged. Escape soon, rely on distracting the guards' attention and do the unexpected.

Nowhere is exploitation of the unexpected better demonstrated than in Oflag VIIc – Colditz. The idea of building a glider to fly to freedom is unprecedented, if you discount the mythic escape of Icarus and Daedalus. Even the hiding place of the secret glider was extraordinary. Instead of taking the plane apart and hiding it under floorboards the prisoners built an *entirely false wall* at one end of an attic, so creating the space for a secret workshop.

When the French started a tunnel they counter-intuitively put the entrance in the clock tower – *at the very top*. It was an incredibly successful idea. Even though the Germans could hear tunnelling they could never find out where. As in many wartime adventures the human element was the deciding factor. Though the Germans used sophisticated listening equipment, they only found the French tunnel when a loose-tongued former tunneller boasted of it to an informer at a new camp he was transferred to.

One, almost perfect, Colditz escape started from the recreation ground. In the field's centre was a drain hole with a manhole cover locked and bolted on the outside. If a prisoner managed to pick the lock, hide in the drain and his colleagues managed to lock him in (the lock was always inspected by the guards before the prisoners left the field), he would still be unable to escape because he couldn't unlock the cover from the inside. The Dutch contingent worked a way around it – by painting a glass aspirin tube black they were able to substitute a glass bolt for the real one. After the guards had left it only took a sturdy heave to break the glass and climb free. Then, in a real stroke of genius, the escaping prisoner brushed up the glass and replaced the real bolt. Houdini couldn't have managed it better.

46 Make a hunting knife from an old file

It's all very well buying things, but nothing gives more pleasure than making something that others assume just has to be bought. Knives are one such thing. They may look hard to make, but with a little ingenuity and time you can turn out a knife superior or equal to any you can buy.

First get hold of an old file from a car boot sale or junk shop. One about eight inches long is fine. Next, using bricks or a barbecue stand, build a mini-forge. This just has to be a place to hold charcoal. Get it going so that you have a good big bed of embers. Obtain a bicycle pump, or better, one of those plastic hand pumps used to blow up rubber boats. Fit a piece of garden hose to it and get a friend or a useful infant to pump it – thus blowing air into your 'forge'. If this all sounds too technical wait until a really windy day, build the barbecue behind a line of bricks, then remove one so the wind gets the embers really red hot.

Using pliers lay the file in the embers and wait for it to glow red hot, cherry red in fact. When it has reached this stage, draw it from the fire and cool it slowly by placing it into a bucket of ashes or a pile of sand. The 'temper' or hardness of the file will now be gone and you can work it like any other piece of softish metal. Saw the end with a hacksaw to make a vague point, then file like crazy to make the edge of the blade and to smooth the shape of the knife. This takes an age, but is worth it. Drill two holes (you can use a hand drill, but a power drill is easier), one through the tang (the handle point of the file) and one low down at the end near the tang.

Now you have the basic outline of a knife it's time to shape it. Use coarse and fine files to get the design you want along with as sharp a blade as you can manage. Now heat the blade in the forge until it's cherry red again. Take it out and plunge it into a can of oil to cool (or water, but oil is better). Then put the blade in your oven and set the temperature to high. Keep an eye on the blade, checking its colour from time to time. When you see the steel going a straw colour, remove it from the oven and plunge it into water to cool it off. The blade is now both toughened and hardened enough to be a useful knife.

Glue sheets of coarse, medium and fine Carborundam paper (the black sandpaper) to a piece of glass. Sand the blade flat on all three surfaces getting finer as you go. Angle the edge and sand that, too.

Using the smooth paper polish the blade as much as you can. Then use a coarse Japanese water stone to wear the edge to a sharpness. Follow with a medium and then a fine stone.

To make a handle, hollow out a piece of hardwood so that the tang fits snugly in the wood. Carve away wood so that the file goes halfway down the handle with the tang taking the rest of the length. Drill the handle to match the holes in the file. Get an old die-cast metal toy car and melt it in a shoe polish tin in your fire. Pour the molten metal into the holes to seal the handle on. Otherwise use bolts and countersunk nuts to fasten it together. In the absence of that, use wire to bind the entire handle.

Sharpen again and strop a hundred times each side on a piece of thick leather. Test for sharpness by cutting the wetted hairs on the back of your wrist. Fashion a sheath from a discarded piece of stout leather.

47 Assassinate the despotic leader of an evil regime at 500 metres

If you are familiar with *Rogue Male*, the book and the film, you'll know its unforgettable premise is a botched attempt on Hitler's life by a sporting deer-hunter training his sights on the Nazi leader. Now, if, just if, he had been successful, then maybe the Second World War could have been avoided.

Assassination is a nasty subject. Most governments do not condone its use, at least not openly. However, let us imagine a tyrant like Saddam Hussein: surely a lot of time and trouble could have been saved by taking a pot shot at him?

And what if it fell to you: how would you go about hitting your man at 500m or perhaps even more?

First off, all successful rifle-shooting is about controlling your breathing and your heartbeat. The better you play dead the better you'll shoot. Eye is, of course, necessary, but many people have a good eye and a steady hand. How many are so ice cold their body hardly registers its own pulse?

It is managed, ice in the veins that is, by a combination of holding your breath and not caring about the result of the shot. It's very Zen – the moment you really care if you hit the bull's-eye or not your pulse begins to strain at your arm and wrist and the rifle bumps a millimetre, less than a millimetre, but multiply that by 500m and you've missed, as good as by a mile.

One trick is in holding your breath without noticing, almost as an afterthought. Don't take any kind of preliminary in-breath; don't give yourself any warning. Just stop breathing; kind of put a lock on your chest rather than gulping and slamming your mouth shut. Feel you heart disappearing into your interior, exhale with your body, except without breathing if that makes sense.

The next level up is to learn how to fire between heartbeats – so the slower your pulse the better. Holding your breath will slow the pulse under normal conditions. Practise getting your own rhythm of aiming and sensing your heartbeat and slip the trigger in the half-second gap you have between beats. This will take a lot of practice. It helps to have a Zen-like attitude with no attachment to any outcome. Fire with care, but as if you couldn't care less.

The rest is mostly technical. Rain and humidity affect range, as do light and, of course, a following wind or a headwind. Make adjustments and dial in the altered range by turning the elevation knob on top of the sights in 100m increments. You dial in lateral changes on the side knob. If you are on a range you'd be allowed several shots to get your sights in – when you assassinate a tyrant you won't get that chance. If the day you planned to shoot is thundery you have a problem – lower air pressure can mean up to a metre difference in elevation at half a kilometre. Even the difference between a sunny and a cloudy day will affect your shooting: if the sky is clear you need less elevation than if it's cloudy – at 500 metres this can amount to 20cm difference on the target.

A few final tips: if the wind just tingles the hairs on your arm it's going only 1–3mph. If it's 3–5mph it'll divert a pinch of dirt dropped from the hand; 5–7mph and it will make a cloth flap; 7–10mph and it will cause leaves and grass to rustle; anything above 10mph and your chances of a miss at long range increase. If you aim into a valley the target will look closer. If you aim onto a hill, further away.

Ideally, then, you will sight your rifle in at the correct range and as near in time and place to the actual site of the shooting as possible. And remember: keep your eye a good way back from the telescopic sight as the recoil can give you a nasty cut.

Choice of weapon: Lee Harvey Oswald assassinated Kennedy (not that this was the kind of assassination we have in mind) using a Mannlicher Caracano carbine, a short Italian rifle built between 1891 and 1940 – hardly a space-age weapon. He used a cheap four-power telescope – the kind that nowadays might be fitted to a child's first air rifle. With this equipment he fired a rather weak 6.5mm Italian cartridge – still deadly accurate in the hands of a trained marksman such as Oswald, who was shooting from a mere 80m away.

Tyrants are more paranoid than democrats, which is why you, as the putative assassin of a second Hitler, will need to be able to shoot at a distance of 500m or more. A good choice of rifle would be the Finnish Sako TRG, which fires a high power .338 Lapua Magnum round. The rifle favoured for sniper duty in Vietnam was the Remington 700 chambered for a 7.62mm boat-tail bullet, which, with its tapered base, was more accurate than a square-cut bullet. Alternatively, and this is the British Army sniper's weapon of choice, you might choose the Accuracy International L96A1 Long Range rifle chambered for a 7mm Remington magnum round.

The important thing about highly accurate rifles is that the barrel needs to be free floating, with something like 0.5mm or less clearance from the stock of the gun. Once the bullet is fired and travels down the barrel it has no more contact. With fixed barrels the transit of each bullet knocks the sights slightly out of alignment and to be really accurate they need adjusting much more often.

Any of the above would be a conventional, and very good, choice. However, if the weapon does not need to be hiked a long distance then there is the alternative of a large calibre sniping rifle, designed for taking out helicopter rotors, antennae or detonating explosives at a distance. The Barrett M82A2 is a bullpup design (magazine behind the trigger), which makes it less cumbersome than a traditional shaped rifle, though it still weighs a heavy 12kg. It fires the powerful .50in calibre Browning round that can penetrate an inch of steel at 500m. Overkill? If your target is wearing protective armour then it might be necessary to use such a powerful long-range weapon.

Even more specialised, and the holder of the longest confirmed sniper kill, is the McMillan TAC-50 rifle. The TAC-50 weighs a hefty 11.79kg, has a heavy, free-floating barrel and is fitted with 16× power Leupold telescopic sights. It can shoot a centimetre-sized group at 100m. Used by Canadian corporal Rob Furlong in Afghanistan, he killed a member of the Taliban at 2,450m. That beat the previous record held by US marine sniper Carlos Hathcock, who had a confirmed kill in Vietnam of 2,286m or 1.42 miles. This was using a Browning machine gun 0.50 calibre with a telescopic sight. Some argue that Hathcock's jungle shot is still the more impressive as Furlong was shooting at 9,000ft above sea level. When the air is thinner the drag on the bullet is less, thus making longer shots more accurate. Either way, shooting someone from over two kilometres away is an extraordinary feat. If your tyrant dictator is especially paranoid or well-guarded you may want to consider using a .50 calibre long-range weapon.

Finally the getaway. In *Rogue Male* the hero is captured, beaten and left for dead, but survives to fight another day. In your fantasy assassination of an evil tyrant you don't want to get killed making your escape. Set up a decoy – a fake sniper's nest at a closer distance, maybe a car with a rifle protruding from a hole in the boot. You can set this up with a simple radio control servo to fire without any degree of accuracy after you have delivered the kill shot. Make sure the rifle is a semi-automatic with a thirty-round magazine – a Ruger Mini 14 would be fine. The close protection squad will focus their attention on destroying this target, allowing you to make your escape hidden beneath a secret panel in a tow truck pulling an apparently broken-down ambulance. No one ever stops tow trucks on hospital business.

48 How to rise to the top of any corporation – fast

Corporations are not about fairness, competence, efficiency, loyalty, giving minorities a chance, being a team player, building a sense of community, making a better world or donating time and money to charity. Corporations are about two things only: power and, at one remove, money.

Note which way round these are. Money isn't first. If money came first – as it does among salesmen, entrepreneurs and the self-employed – then new ideas would be welcomed if they had money-making potential. But we all know that new ideas are mostly unwelcome in corporations, even though they need a certain number of old ideas dressed up as new ones to keep going.

Money follows from power. You get to be the boss and you get stock options and bonuses and everything else that makes you very, very rich and loathed by most normal people. Is it simple envy? I don't think so. People don't loathe very wealthy footballers and popstars with nearly the same degree of venom. Footballers actually do something. They do what they are supposed to do extremely well. Corporate bosses, while prating about their 'great product', we all know very well are merely doing everything they can to (a) hang onto their job; (b) get promoted; and (c) obtain even more power.

Performance doesn't lead to promotion. The possibility of promotion causes 'performance-type simulations' to be created. We all know them: cost cutting, getting in consultants and then firing people, merging or selling off real estate. That's what corporations mainly do. Along the way they incidentally make cars, video cameras, movies and money for the stockholders.

This is a gross exaggeration but it is the right perspective. If you join a car corporation thinking you are here to make marvellous cars, you will be sorely frustrated. You are there to build a power base that slowly propels you upwards into the realm of VIP washrooms and Gulfstream VI jets.

These days you should not stand out in the corporate world; your power must be amorphous. You should be known for one thing only: frightening efficiency. If you have twenty-three tasks on your to-do list you get them done. You are never late except intentionally to emphasise your power. You are polite and friendly to all. If you appear in the trades it's for two things only: raising money for charity or for a promotion.

Get your tame man – someone loyally in your pocket, or deeply in fear of you because of the compromising photos taken at the Christmas party which are in your possession – to talk to the press. Figureheads higher up resent those lower down hogging the limelight. The best press is the namecheck. That's where your man comes in: he is quoted, but it's your project and name that are mentioned.

At work the real work is done before anyone gets there and after everyone has left. Work time is power time. Your object is to increase office space, the number of employees and your responsibilities – you must always be looking for more work. But here's the trick: it doesn't have to be done that well; merely on time and good enough. Get too involved in doing a 'good job' and you'll over-run your schedule. It's impossible to do real work in an office environment – which is actually designed for spying on employees and facilitating power games. Therefore do the real work at home or very early in the morning. Always get to work early and leave late – that way you'll hear of any intrigues. Never announce you are 'working from home'. Always be in the office.

Learn to be very wary of innovation. Most new things fail. To be associated with failure requires a job shift, which is no bad thing; you should be shifting every two or three years within a corporation – if not move upwards outside it. How often you company hop depends on the industry. Identify high flyers within your profession and see how often they switch jobs. As I said, beware of innovation and its even more toxic relative 'creativity'. Both of those are associated in the corporate group mind with expensive failures like Howard Hughes' Spruce Goose airplane or Clive Sinclair's C5 electric trolley.

Learn, however, how to steal or otherwise appropriate something that obviously works but which is being mismanaged by a creative type. Make it yours, but allow your power team to disseminate the propaganda – don't blow your own trumpet. As the Japanese say, the nail that sticks out sooner or later gets hammered.

Your power team are important. These are folks who not only owe you one – that's not enough – but who you also have something on. It can be very small, but just enough to put the fear into them. You know their weaknesses. You know what lies they have on their résumé. You encourage their loose talk and then you remember.

100

People should be scared of you. Nice guys finish last. How you scare people without making them hate and resist you is one of the great skills of the corporate world. Make sure your hobby is macho, but not considered silly like karate or judo. Join an exclusive rifle-shooting club. You don't have to go often. A well-liked boss is usually a little scary, a little bit strict. Be very fair but have a reputation as a mass firer. Do other people's firing for them – it's actually psychologically easier than firing your own people. Go out and face large public meetings where you have to announce shutting down the only source of work in that town. Go in fighting and expect tough opposition, but after the meeting talk to every one of the people who attacked you from the floor in person. One on one they will be flattered to be talking to the top man. They will be your ambassadors, saying that the company is a bitch but that you're OK and opposition will falter. Inside the company your *cojones* will be revered.

Understand the secret power structure of the corporation. This is maintained by those who have stubbornly remained all their working lives in the same company, sometimes even in the same job. Their power is information and timing. They know when to strike and when to hold back as they have an intuitive experiential grasp of the inevitable cycles of any company. They know everyone and all the gossip. These old-timers or long-timers need to be recruited. They can be vastly useful. Since they can see through your transparent ascent to power you have to protect them, encourage their pet projects and, above all, be friendly and respectful to them. Their reward is getting their own little plans encouraged, their own *idée fixe* agreed with. Once one is on your side, conquer his network of secret power – his long-timer friends above and below will be very useful.

Use the power of obligation to get your own way. Find out

and keep lists of the hobbies, obsessions and interests of those you wish to influence. When you see something irresistible – a rare book by their favourite author, a toy for their kids, inside information they could use – give of it generously and expect and actually discourage any reciprocation. Wait until you need something important – then ask.

Pass the time of day with timewasters who have power – the ordinary 'hardworkers' will be cut out of such profitable behaviour. Catch up after hours.

Encourage the promotion of childless women in their late thirties. Get a name for fairness if not outright feminism. Recommend to others in power women to be offered jobs even you aspire to. A good 50 per cent will soon be pregnant – biology is your unwitting agent here – and as soon as they take their six-week leave move in and appropriate their power with their consent; you are just being considerate in this time of stress. Consolidate your powers during periods of postnatal depression. Make the most of divorce – in others – to appropriate yet more power.

But isn't all this disgusting amoral behaviour? Ah, well, if morality is your main concern, seek not employment in the cut and thrust world of big bad business …

49 Get your blades razor sharp

Sharpening a knife defeats even skilful DIYers. It is an old skill, fallen somewhat into disuse. Yet it is essential for getting any pleasure out of an edged tool of any kind. Any old stone can be used for sharpening. The smoother it is the longer it takes, but the finer the resulting edge. Like polishing shoes, with enough time any blade can be made super sharp.

Using Japanese water stones makes sharpening a lot easier. These stones, after immersion in water, wear steel away faster than oilstones. Use a circling or a back and forth movement – doing equal work on both sides. It doesn't matter so much as long as you keep the blade at broadly the same angle to the stone. Examine the blade through a magnifying glass to learn what each stroke against the stone is doing to the metal edge. When you have an idea of what the stone does your sharpening will improve greatly.

By starting with coarse stones and moving to a finer one you will get an edge that shines rather than one that looks scratched – that is the sign of a truly sharp blade. Next strop the blade against a stout leather belt to smooth the edge without ripping out small pieces of metal. Test by cutting paper using the blade's own weight or clipping wet hairs off the back of your wrist.

50 Start Guy Fawkes Night with flair

November the fifth is a time when pyromaniacs of all ages can unleash their love of flame. To start the evening in a way guaranteed to be great fun and much appreciated by all, especially the kids, do the following.

Make a pile of sawdust within the lower space of the bonfire, douse this with petrol. Take a long roll of smooth garden wire and affix it to any sturdy log well inside the bonfire structure.

Uncoil the wire until you have reached a tree you can climb or better a treehouse. Attach the wire so it is straight and tight and aiming into the fire.

Take a medium-sized rocket and make two rings of wire around it and two smaller circles of wire to go around the guide wire. Test that the rocket can slide smoothly along the wire and that it is very firmly held by the wire cradle. Tape the cradle on if necessary.

Night falls. Light an Olympic flame (alright, a stick wound with sack soaked in diesel oil) and carry this through the crowd aloft, triumphant. Pass this up the tree to the treehouse to your pyro-pal. He lights the rocket. Stand well back and watch it shoot down the wire into the fire. Its back blast should catch the sawdust and the whole bonfire will then burst into flame. When the rocket explodes it will be safely contained by the bonfire.

51 Be king of the barbecue

Becoming barbecue royalty is not difficult, but does require some preparation, both in making the fire and in preparing the meat.

Most barbies are started too late, have the grill too close and result in meat that is both under- and overcooked at the same time. I'm not talking about gas barbecues, which are nothing more than outdoor cookers and hardly worth bothering with. A real barbie is always charcoal or wood. If it is wood then you must allow at least an hour plus for the right quantity of embers to build up. Use hard wood if you can as it burns much slower and generates more heat.

For most of us, though, it's charcoal: get the real kind and not the briquettes, which can impart a kerosene odour to the meat. Start with firestarters or paper and leave for forty minutes to get a decent bed of really hot charcoal. Now grade this so that you have very hot at one end and only slightly hot/quite warm at the other. Make sure you can raise and lower the grill to your taste.

Now the meat. The whole thing is in the quality of the beef or lamb and the marinading time. Prepare a flat dish of barbecue sauce, several tablespoons of vinegar, lashings of olive oil, soy sauce, several crushed cloves of garlic, pepper, beer or wine. Immerse the meat overnight – be it steak or lamb chop. Adjust the sauce to your taste, being only a bit careful not to overuse the vinegar.

On B-Day remove the meat and salt both sides well – a teaspoon for each large steak is not too much. Rub in well. Use a hamburger to gauge the heat of your barbecue if you are unsure. Lower the grill so that the burger turns brown quickly but doesn't burn. Lay down the steaks and cook for two minutes a side max. Chops can take even less unless you are addicted to well-done meat.

---

52 How to make an elephant vanish

You know that all those large-scale conjuring tricks by David Copperfield and other stage magicians are done with smoke and mirrors – but it still *looks like* magic. Just how is a mirror used to make something disappear?

The first thing is that the magician must be able to control your point of view. That's especially easy with TV as you just keep the camera in one place. Likewise an audience stays where it is seated in the theatre. If you can move you can get past the small range in which the mirrors work.

The next principle is a uniform background and sideground, so to speak. A plain curtain running right around the back and sides of the stage is fine. Now comes the trick. The mirror reflects a piece of background, which because of uniformity looks just like what should be there anyway.

To clarify: if I roll on a cabinet with sides I can lift, it can have a mirror on either side that reflects the opposite view, which is identical to the view behind it. Therefore it looks as if there is nothing there. All such cabinets have frames around such 'nothingness' so that you can't see the edge of the mirror. Behind the angled mirror you hide your assistant or your elephant.

You can see now how the lady sawing works: you actually have a mirror at the end of the cabinet which makes it look empty – in fact a girl is curled up there. When you bolt in your assistant it is the secret helper who shows her legs and your assistant who has hers pulled up. This allows for the saw and for the separated wiggling feet.

To make something as big as an elephant disappear, all you need is a big mirror and clever stagecraft. First wheel in a gigantic three-legged table; rising from it is a rail with a circular curtain, a bit like the curtain you draw around hospital beds. Get the audience to look underneath it and pronounce it normal. Draw the curtains around it with a volunteer on top – then draw them back to reveal they are still there. The elephant is then paraded across the stage. Get the elephant to climb onto the table. The curtain, when drawn, allows a clear view under the table. People to the side can see behind the table. There is a blast of trumpets and the curtain is drawn back – the elephant has vanished!

When the elephant is paraded in front of the table it blocks the view of the table long enough to cover the rise of two giant angled mirrors from the floor which diverge from the front leg to the two side legs and reflect the curtains on either side. This allows a 'V'-shaped space that covers the rise of a giant elevator platform from the floor which connects to the middle part of the table and lowers the elephant under the stage. It then rises back up and replaces it in position.

During all this potentially noisy elevation a group from the audience are being instructed in playing giant flugelhorns, 'elephant' horns designed to aid the magic, along with recorded trumpeting noises.

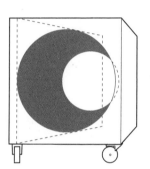

Houdini's Vanishing Elephant Cabinet from the front

Houdini's Vanishing Elephant Cabinet from the top

53 Mummify a dear departed friend

Home mummification may be something of a niche activity, but in this age of eco-burials in biodegradable coffins and shooting loved one's ashes into space, why not?

First obtain your corpse. It might be advisable to start on a pet – ducks are quite popular as mummification test pieces, but you could try a cat, a dog or even a hamster.

Two-and-a-half thousand years ago, Herodotus, a source for much of our knowledge about ancient Egypt, wrote that there were three methods of mummification depending on wealth and class and no doubt similar reasons that distinguish nowadays between a paupers' grave or a state funeral. 'The most perfect practice is to extract with an iron hook as much of the brain as possible and what the hook cannot reach rinse the remainder out with special drugs. Next the flank is laid open with a flint knife and the whole contents of the abdomen removed. The cavity is cleansed and washed with palm wine and an infusion of spices. Then the body is filled up with bruised myrrh, cassia and every other aromatic substance except frankincense, sewn up and the whole body placed in natron and covered over for never more than seventy days.'

Natron was a mineral salt freely and naturally available in Egypt – a mix of sodium bicarbonate and calcium carbonate.

There is no doubt that the idea of mummification came from the desert. Very early predyastic tombs reveal natural mummies, ones that have been desiccated perfectly by the extreme aridity of the desert. Once the Nile became the centre of Egyptian civilisation it was too humid to merely leave a body – it would decompose. And so the elaborate methods of preservation were developed.

Herodotus again: 'When, for reasons of expense, the second quality is called for. The treatment is different: no incision and the intestines are not removed. Instead oil of cedar is injected into the anus which is then firmly stopped up to stop it escaping. The body is then dry salted with natron and left for the prescribed number of days. The anus is then unstoppered and the oil is so powerful it brings out the intestines and stomach in a liquid state.' That's certainly one to try first on a small rodent or even a budgie before employing it on a dear departed human friend.

Lastly Herodotus speaks of the poor: 'The third method, for those with no wealth, is to simply clean out the intestines with a purge and keep the body seventy days on natron.'

To get a little more technical and to use a method based on the 'royal' technique, one should puncture a hole in the ethnoid bone at the inside upper end of the nose, the one that separates the brain from the sinuses. Through this small opening one can draw out the contents of the brain without leaving any disfiguring marks. Any bits of brain left behind can be swilled out with aromatic wine – retsina is the closest thing we have to that and works rather well.

The removed body parts need to be stored in a mixture of sodium carbonate and sodium bicarbonate – natron. Fill the body with the same substance and leave for four weeks. Now the body is washed of its salts and packed with linen to restore its shape.

You can fashion a good brain hook from an old bicycle spoke. Sodium carbonate can be obtained in the form of washing soda from any traditional hardware store. Bicarbonate you can buy in any supermarket. Mix the two in proportion: two parts soda to one part bicarbonate. To obtain linen packing I suggest a visit to a charity shop – you will find old women's blouses and jackets made of linen and for a cheap price.

The abdominal incision is covered with a leather plate decorated with the eye of Horus. Plug the eye sockets with linen, or, better, with artificial eyes. The ancient Egyptians were masters at making realistic artificial eyeballs; they used naturally occurring silica glass from the Sahara desert for this purpose – the world's first glass eyes. Rub spices and resins over the body and chant some incantations. All variety of unguents can be used. Pine-based pitch and resin help to preserve the body better and give the bandages something to stick to.

Obtain a goodly length of bandage. Linen lasts longest, though cotton will do at a pinch. Start at the fingers and toes with narrow bandage and then move up the limbs and finally to the body. Intersperse within the bandages amulets and scarabs. A scarab should lie directly over the heart – the only organ that remains within the mummy. Inscribed on the heart scarab should be an incantation not to bear hostile witness to the deceased, i.e., don't badmouth the dead even after you've dug them up and put them on show in a museum. Outer layers of bandages, some of them in different colours, are an optional extra for fancy mummies. Place your mummy in a case made from the traditional material known as cartonnage. This is just papier-mâché, so perhaps you can encourage local primary school kids to give you hand with this.

Four canopic jars must be stored with the mummy. These contain the stomach, whose sign is a jackal; the intestines, whose sign is a falcon; the lungs (ape); and the liver, whose sign is a human being – perhaps an ancient Egyptian nod at their great appetite for beer and palm wine. Finally place in a giant stone box or sarcophagus for burial.

For the interested amateur animals provide useful training. The ancient Egyptians also mummified everything from cats to crocodiles so there is a reliable precedent. The method is the same – brain hooking and intestine removal. Once the animal has been eviscerated, wash it out with retsina and cover with a mixture of melted violin rosin and beeswax or any aromatic wax. For bandages, cut up old sheets or, if feeling extravagant, use real bandages.

Mummified cats and ducks make good conversation pieces if displayed well in a glass cabinet. To maintain adequate dryness, you can hang plastic dehumidifiers discreetly in your cabinet.

54 How to buy a second hand car in the Third World without getting ripped off

When it comes to car buying in countries renowned for rip-offs and dodginess even the stoutest hearted among us begins to quiver and quake – what if it's a lemon? What if the clutch drops out after 50 miles? I'm no mechanic.

You don't have to be a mechanic to buy a good car anywhere in the world; you just have to be able to read people and understand some simple principles. Firstly, you buy the owner not the car. If the man selling it is a sly, unreliable and untrustworthy git then chances are the car will be too. A solid and reliable citizen will have looked after his motor. The person you really seek is the enthusiast. This is why it pays to buy a car with collectorish overtones, an enthusiast's car. In most Third World countries there exists a rich elite who delight in the childish pleasures of off-roading or rallying – these people are often a good source of a reliable motor. Don't expect to get one cheap, but at least it will work.

Look under the engine bay – is it clean? Are fluids topped up? As for rust – if there is any it probably doesn't matter unless it is under the doors and in the wheel arches. Scratch the chassis if you're buying a 4x4 and check if you can see metal. If the car has ever been in an accident then you probably shouldn't buy it. If you do, take it to a vehicle alignment centre (a tyre centre can do it cheaply) and check the wheels are the same distance apart – if they have such a place that is. More basic tests include seeing whether it veers to one side while driving.

Check for weird noises – thudding, clicking, squeaking or vibrating. A good car makes a happy noise reminiscent of a favourite uncle humming along to the theme from *The Dam Busters*. A bad car is hard to listen to; like a screaming infant it begs to be abandoned or mistreated in some inexcusable way. Zone into your inner quality detector: if it feels good to drive, buy it without fear.

You may be faced with a smiling face trying to peddle something that probably needs peddles as well as an engine. Cheap spares and labour are your trump card here; your enemy is the poorly constructed cheap import that has been badly maintained. In Africa, Peugeot have a huge distribution of spare parts. There is also the local knowledge to fix them. VW camper wagons are used in the Third World not to ferry celebrity chefs around but as working microbuses. You may buy one that is knackered, but you can be sure you can get it fixed and parts replaced cheaply. Cars with good build quality are your best bet in the Third World: old Mercs, Toyotas and Peugeot 504s. Avoid Land Rovers and Jeeps: they look tough, but that look just encourages lack of care in the Third World. Most are so knackered as to need constant coddling and repair. Russian and Eastern bloc motors, and anything from China or Korea, should also be given short shrift. For some reason the superpowers – Russia, China and America – have never made reliable motors.

As for bargaining, prepare to be asked for amazing, greed-fuelled, insane prices for something you wouldn't donate to *Scrapheap Challenge*. Prepare to be offended by the sheer ludicrousness of such demands, though actually your best bet is just to laugh. It is much much better to know the going rate already and if no money is mentioned to announce that is what you will pay. Don't budge, or budge a tiny fraction. Be prepared to walk away, do it too. If the guy knows his stuff he will clock you know your stuff (i.e., the correct price) and you will not be overcharged. Although they may try it on in a different way – charge a lot for some changes you might need, new tyres or a re-spray. It is better to buy the car and get it renovated elsewhere. To find out the correct price is not always easy. Many people are so inflamed with greed that every advert is actually wildly optimistic. You have to find what people really paid. Often you find people selling in a hurry for a big discount. Foreigners leaving the country may also need to sell and you can buy cheaply from them.

Never be in a hurry to buy even if you are. Inhabitants of the Third World can smell desperation, they've grown up with it, they are attuned to it.

Last tip. If you don't know the owner, do not let the car out of your sight after you have paid the money. One friend bought a Hyundai 4x4 in Morocco. In the three hours between paying and picking the thing up, the nearly new engine he'd seen and approved had been switched for a knackered piece of vibrating debris.

55 General Rommel's secrets of success

1 Everyday do something you find physically painful and unpleasant. Rommel always rose at 6 a.m. and ran for 1km flat out, even when he had chest pains and was diagnosed with heart problems in his late forties. His reasoning was that though he hated running in the early morning, 'I detested it,' he wrote, it meant he kept his discipline in trim.

2 Never be tired, never eat and never sleep – at least not in public. Nothing inspires troops more than being led by a superman. Eat and drink in private, at odd times and always refuse sustenance in public. Learn as Rommel did to take twenty-minute naps every three hours or so.

3 Minimise losses by tactics rather than maximise gains. Rather than waste men gaining a mile of ground, settle for gaining 500 yards with minimum losses. Find out what is possible with the men you have and achieve it. Great gains with major losses will mean no men to achieve something the next day. To generalise into business: look after the downside and the upside will look after itself.

4 Reconnoitre in force. Rommel turned his fortunes in North Africa after losing 386 of his 412 tanks in January 1941 and after two-thirds of the Axis armies had been destroyed. Just when he would have been expected to retreat he decided to reconnoitre the enemy in force. Catching the previously victorious army off guard, he captured a hundred tanks and returned the front line to its former position. Reconnaissance in force allows you to make the most of any mistake the enemy may make.

5 Which leads us to rule number five: be merciless on any mistake made by the enemy. Mercy has its place in war,

but only after prisoners have been captured or a surrender has been negotiated. There is no better way to weaken morale than to stamp heavily and loudly on every mistake the enemy makes, because he will then blame his own command and direct his energy inwards rather than outwards at his real attackers.

6 Promote enthusiasm, spirit and correct values ahead of specialised skills, physical fitness and military training. In combat one can more easily teach military skills to an enthusiastic leader than leadership and enthusiasm to someone who knows drill and rifle maintenance.

7 Carry on an attack regardless of what is happening in your rear … in both senses – Rommel both ignored internal complaints such as jaundice, food poisoning and diarrhoea when at war and more importantly taught his troops not to fight while looking over their shoulders. A well-planned attack will not be left unprotected, trust in the attack and keep focused. With enough momentum, one is usually never cut off. Being encircled is usually the fate of an army that does not move forward fast enough.

8 Chose fairness over popularity every time. Easy to say, but hard to do. Rommel was famous for not caring how popular he was with his officers, but he was always scrupulously fair. Over time the reputation for fairness will undermine the need for superficial popularity.

9 Use tanks en masse and not in tiny packets. To generalise, understand that each arm has an optimum size and that by supporting itself it then maximises its impact. The British never really grasped this and very often deployed tanks in too small groups; too small to make any real impact, they were picked off one by one.

10 Trust your intuition in the midst of battle. Things move too fast and are too confusing in battle to process information slowly and rationally. Instead you have to lock

into the rhythm of the battle and become dynamically engaged, never stopping but always making decision after decision as soon as it seems wise, never double-checking, never hesitating. War is not a science and in a fluid situation keeping moving is paramount. Rather as in football one is best served by keeping the ball in play even if it means passing backwards, so, too the momentum of instinctive leadership in confusing battle scenarios permits a flexible response that enables one to keep acting until the action is at an end.

11 A disordered enemy does not protect his flanks. If one can harass and disrupt an enemy and get them on the run, both mentally and physically, one can take the calculated and justified risk that they will not protect themselves from attack on either side – they will be too concerned about what is coming at them from the front (or rear if they are already running).

56 Buying an old and leaky boat

In a word, don't. No one needs a boat, except fishermen. You don't need a boat. You want a boat, we all do. If not a yacht like Onassis at least a dinghy with sails or a nice little outboard. Boats are nice to think about. They increase your zone of possibility. They are lovely to look at in a harbour, their mast halyards all clicking in the wind.

Don't do it. Don't buy that boat. It'll eat money like a Vegas slot machine; it'll give you more heartache than teenage love with sleepless nights when you lie awake mouthing words like 'must haul out' and 'mooring fees'. It isn't the boat that's your problem (well it is, but that's not the half of it), it's what comes with the boat – maintenance, keeping it somewhere, visiting it.

A wiser man than I once told me: 'After long study of the matter I've come to the conclusion that there is no such thing as a cheap boat.' There are boats with a low price tag, but these are not 'cheap' in the usually acceptable meaning of the word. Not once you've budgeted in the time, paint, trouble, the hauling out and putting in, the leaks and the rot – both dry and wet. No, when you add all that in you have a very expensive boat indeed. And double it if you have mooring fees.

A good rule is never to buy a boat that is out of the water. First, why is it out of its natural environment? That should make you suspicious. Cheap boats are rarely in the water. Often they look quite nice on dry land sitting on a tailor-made trailer: do not be tempted. Tell the owner you want to see it in the water first. If he blanches or refuses, walk away. A boat that has been long years out of water and has cracks in its bottom you can see through do not buy. There are a lot of boats like that – I once bought one – and I, too, never got it in the water. That was a cheap boat. I must have spent four times at least what I paid for it on all the repairs and fees. In the end I sold it to another dreamer for exactly what I paid for it.

Did I learn? No way. I made one slight improvement; I bought one that was in the water this time, but it was so far away from where I lived that just visiting the boat cost me a tank-full of petrol and so that cheap boat turned out expensive too.

Still not convinced? Alright. This is what I know. Forget the sailing mags and the boat books; they're written by enthusiasts, deluded fools, but you won't be deluded for ever. You want to go sailing not painting and scrubbing. You need a fibreglass boat. Sorry, it has no charm like teak and pitch pine, it has no strength of character like steel, it doesn't even have the weirdness of concrete, but that's what you want. An old, well-made, well looked after fibreglass boat – one that has been made in thousands and is deeply unfashionable but is known not to sink.

If it has a lovely working engine then great and expect to pay extra for that. If it only has an outboard, that's even better – less to go wrong and easier to fix. Check the rigging and the quality of the sails: are they all baggy? If you're spending more than £2,000 employ a surveyor to give it a look – the yacht mags are full of ads for them. A boat isn't like a car: peace of mind matters more with boats, especially in a gale off Dogger Bank. Find out from the mags what the standard price for that age and model of boat is and expect to pay towards the top end for a superior, well cared for example. As with cars, study the owners – try and buy from real enthusiasts who know their onions. Get a boat that's in the water or can be tested and which can be put in the water direct from its trailer. Store it on its trailer as well so you can save mooring fees.

You still want that leaky old traditional boat, don't you? That old cutter or yawl with its hallowed pedigree and hundred-year-old hull? You've seen it going cheap in the pages of *Classic Boat* and can't resist. Alright, do it, but be warned. Be warned! If you can't afford a surveyor or are afraid he will dissuade you from such a foolhardy purchase, here are the basics. How much water is in the bilges? All boats leak, especially all wooden boats. The question is simply: how much. A little over months is nothing. A lot over a short sea trip is worrying.

Is it rotten? Most are, in places. Take a screwdriver and stick it everywhere. Is there a funny smell down below? This is not meant to be facetious: I mean apart from the oily, fishy smell of the bilges, is there a woody, funky, nasty smell of rot? Poke well and hard: your life may depend on it.

What's the rigging like? Sagging and corroded? Are the sails torn? Are the halyards worn through? Never mind the lingo: just check and see how much rope will need replacing and how much the supporting wire looks as though it has been eaten through by salt. The engine is a distraction – it's easy to fix marine engines; it's the boat itself that is the hard part.

The main thing is: if the hull doesn't leak too much, is not rotten and has no holes showing light, it may be OK. That's the best anyone can say. In a word: don't do it – hire a boat, borrow one, do a charter, steal one at high tide, anything except become the owner of a siren ship, a terrible mistress that will consume your money and your soul.

57 Swim the Hellespont

Byron did it – why not you? Patrick Leigh Fermor, writer and former Second World War guerrilla leader, swam the Hellespont when he was over sixty. It's a sure-fire test of manhood and a lot less tiring than the Channel, though potentially more risky.

The Hellespont is the narrow channel that separates Europe from Asia in Turkey, about 100 miles southwest of Istanbul, and is named after Helle, the daughter of Arthamus, who drowned here according to the mythology of the Golden Fleece. It is only between 1.5 and 6km wide, but the powerful current that sweeps down it from the Black Sea to the Aegean means you always end up swimming further than the direct distance.

The Hellespont was made famous as an open-air swimming pool in Greek mythology because Leander would swim across every night to visit his lover Hero, who was a girl. So he swam both ways, from Abydos on the Asian side to Sestus on the

European. When Byron lived for a while by the Hellespont he became obsessed with swimming it. He tried in April but it was too cold, so he tried again a month later. Because he wasn't as confident as Leander he set off a mile or so up stream from Abydos, which is very close to the narrowest point. Though Byron had a club foot he was a strong swimmer. He once swam the Thames from Putney Bridge to Westminster – that's a long way in what was then an open sewer. His favoured stroke was the breaststroke. When he made it across the Hellespont he claimed it had taken him seventy minutes and that he was freezing cold. The water moves so swiftly that it is constantly cooling. For your Hellespont swim you might practise in the North Sea just to get acclimatised. Rub in Vaseline and wear a full swim suit. Remember that even a top long-distance swimmer barely exceeds 3km an hour.

For those who want an assured success, there is an annual Hellespont swim organised by the Rotary club of the Turkish town of Canakkale. They even stop the extensive sea traffic for two hours – which is a major blessing as being run down by a tanker is a distinct possibility Byron didn't have to face. The date for this is always 30 August when the Hellespont is at its warmest.

If you want to swim from Leander's spot, Abydos, now called Nagara Point, you must start from a boat – even if it's only a few metres from land and your feet touch the bottom – as this area is now a military zone off limits to eccentric swimmers.

Once you've committed yourself, practise swimming in the sea during rough weather. People who try the Hellespont are often shocked by the waves and the current speed. Wear goggles and a swim hat and you won't get blinded by waves or get so cold. Though many people start off doing the crawl, the breaststroke is hard to beat for a long swim. Not only Byron, but Captain Matthew Webb, the first man to swim the English Channel, swam using the breaststroke. You can keep your eyes open for shipping better, too. Head off directly into the current going at right angles to the other side, even though that seems crazy. You will notice that slowly and painfully you are in fact crossing. When you are halfway you can aim for the other side and the current will help to pull you in quickly. The last 100m is only a metre deep so you can wade out if you are tired.

58 Tricks with car tyres and lighter fuel

Changing a wheel on a car, if you have never done it before, can present certain problems. You can't find the jack. You don't know a safe place to put the jack. The wheel nuts come off, but the wheel seems welded to the hub. If the latter happens, kicking and banging with a hammer should free any seizure. The important thing is to keep the brake on and undo wheel nuts while there is still some contact between the tyre and the ground – that way it won't spin on the axle.

More difficult tests include changing the tyre and not the wheel. How do you get the damn thing off? And then back on again? There are special tyre levers available, but they're seldom around when you really need them. Instead bodge your way using strong flathead screwdrivers, metal chisels and a hammer. Use the hammer and chisel, or hammer and strong screwdriver to 'break the bead' – which just means un-sticking the edge of the tyre from the wheel rim. On inner tube-free tyres this is always a very snug fit. Jump and stamp on the tyre wall to loosen it up. Then hammer and chisel all around and gradually knock the tyre free. Once it is loose use brute strength and several screwdrivers to get it clear of the wheel. Get the new tyre in position by reversing this procedure, but soap up the rim to make sliding the tyre back on easier. Now comes the fun bit. If you just try and inflate the tyre the air will rush out of the gap between tyre and rim. You have to reseat the tyre back on 'the bead'. But hold on – you can't get your chisel inside the tyre can you? One method is to tie a strong cord longitudinally around the tyre, which forces and fattens the tyre out onto the rim. You then pump in air to complete the process. The other more exciting way is to douse the tyre and rim in lighter fuel and spark it alight. The fuel heats the air in the tyre and expands it suddenly; this snaps the tyre back into position on the wheel rim ready to be fully inflated. In really cold weather you can even drive on the tyre without inflating it, using just the hot air inside.

59 Make your own crossbow

The crossbow is a formidable home-build weapon, capable of a good 100 metre-plus range, deadly accurate, and in fact just plain deadly all round. It requires less skill to fire than a long bow and its only disadvantage is its rate of fire. Famously, the French mercenary crossbowmen of Agincourt could only manage two arrows for every sixteen we sent at them with longbows.

The crossbow makes an ideal winter hobby project, possibly suitable as a gift for an energetic teenager with too much testosterone. Or for killing any squirrels, deer, neighbours' cats … I jest. This bow is for demonstration purposes only. Print some targets off Google images.

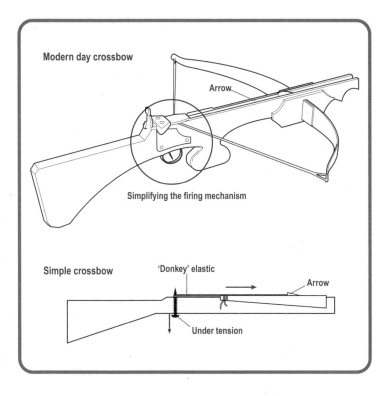

Modern day crossbow

Arrow

Simplifying the firing mechanism

Simple crossbow

'Donkey' elastic

Arrow

Under tension

First you'll need some handy planks of wood and an old car spring. Get along to a scrapyard and root through the boxes of spares to find a leaf spring from an old Escort or similar. Cost – two quid if that. Rush home and spend an infuriating few hours hack-sawing it into a prod shape. The prod is what the bow bit is called on a crossbow. You may not need to saw it if you get a small enough spring, though you will need to shape each end to fix the bow string on. Or you could drill holes. The string is key. You could buy some real bowstring from an archery supply shop online, or you could use linen thread. Take three strands and twist each strand while twisting all three together in the opposite direction. That way when the threads unwind individually they actually wind the composite tighter. Then take each thread of three and wind it with another two of equal gauge. Then take three nine-thread strings and wind those together. Twenty-seven strings should be strong enough but only testing will tell. Use beeswax to make the threads adhere together better. An alternative to winding the bowstring is simply to lay out thirty or more threads and whip them together with a short length of thread sealed with varnish or glue every six inches. It might be easier to buy a ready-made string after all. You can also use wire, for example stainless steel yacht rigging wire.

Using long screws fix the prod to the wooden stock. This is made either from a 2×4 piece of lumber or by gluing and screwing two Ikea bed boards together. Lovingly carve a rifle-shaped stock at one end. Cut a groove in the top for the bolt, which can even be a six-inch nail if you want to be vicious. Otherwise just make a short arrow with flat flights to sit in the groove.

The trigger can be made by drilling a hole upwards at the groove end and inserting a four-inch nail. When you load the crossbow you stand on the prod and pull the string up until it hooks on the nail. Pulling the nail downwards releases the string and thus the bolt. Have the trigger nail loose in its hole and clipped forward with a piece of bent wire (so the point is angled backward holding the string in position). When you rock the nail back like pulling a trigger the string slips off and the bolt is fired. This is the simplest trigger I've made, but you can make them as complicated as you desire.

Bolts can be fashioned from a short length of dowel or any straight stick, such as hazel or ash. You can eliminate any curves by holding the stick while green in the boiling steam of a kettle and then bending it straight. Bind flights cut from a crow's feather, which is best and looks good being black (or any flight feather found while walking in the country), with cobbler's thread. Split the quill using a sharp knife, glue to the bolt shaft and bind front and back with thread. Cut a slight indentation in the shaft to keep the binding from protruding. Trim the feather ends so that the bow string doesn't snag on them. Two flights will work, but three is better: note that the feather must be soft enough to lie flat when the bolt is resting on top of the groove of the crossbow. Or else you might consider cutting a slot down the centre of the groove to accommodate a flight sticking downwards.

You can easily build a cocking device by fixing a bolt through the stock of the crossbow a little way forward of the trigger. Then fashion a piece of curved wood with hooks to fit behind the protruding bolt. This acts as a lever on the bow string, which travels down the curve as the lever is raised up (see diagram).

This crossbow will easily penetrate an inch of wood.

---

60 Climb an unclimbed peak and name it

Despite a generally accepted view that somehow every inch of the world has been explored and discovered, there are in fact hundreds of unclimbed and unnamed mountains just waiting for you to claim their summits. A third of all mountains in eastern Tibet over 6,000m have never been climbed and most have no names, the locals having far better things to do such as finding lost yaks and avoiding conscription into the Chinese army. But for a decadent Westerner with more money than he needs, Tibet is a great place to nail a few truly magnificent 'firsts'. If you are a novice snow and ice climber there are numerous courses one can attend in Scotland or the Alps, but hurry, as you may soon find a lack of snow as global warming wreaks its vengeance on the world of climbing. Once fully confident head out to Tibet and start climbing. The only drawback is that although the Alpine Club will credit you as the first ascendant, the Chinese, who are the current occupying army in Tibet, are reluctant to allow a nasty foreign name to adorn one of 'their' peaks. So you will have to accept their suggestion or simply give it a survey number.

Plan B. The only other major area of unclimbed peaks that don't need huge expertise to climb is Antarctica. Fortunately Antarctica is also owned by no one, having a complicated shared status, though the Americans, with their huge Scott Base at the pole are the most influential. Since the Americans don't recognise any territorial claims to Antarctica it means they also don't recognise anyone else's names, hence the USBGN (United States Board on Geographical Names) subcommittee and the ACAN (Advisory Committee on Antarctic Names). They rule the roost on naming things in Antarctica. Their policy is priority, appropriateness and the extent of establishment of the name's usage.

ACAN are, like all bureaucratic bodies, faintly absurd. They divide the geography of Antarctica into three kinds of nameable features of descending size and importance. First-order features as they call them include 'lands', 'extensive mountain ranges', 'bays' and 'ice shelves'. These can only be named after very famous explorers – the Filchner ice shelf, the Ross Sea or Ellesworth land, for example. Second-order features include 'great or prominent' mountains, peninsulas and small mountain ranges. These can be named after famous Antarctic scientists or people who funded major expeditions in the past, such as Shackleton's financial backer Beardmore, after whom he named a huge glacier. Our interest lies more with the third-order features: 'Minor mountains, cliffs, rocks, points and unprominent glaciers'.

To name a third-order feature you need to have assisted in exploring Antarctica (that's you), been a member of a boat crew used to explore Antarctica or supplied funds that aid in the general exploration of Antarctica.

Should you wish to pass over the egoistic temptation to self-name your find and give a non-personal name to a peak or mountain (important distinction – a mountain may have several peaks all of which can be named as well as naming the mountain) it is preferred that you use a name such as 'hope' point or 'deliverance' bay (both of which have already been taken, but you get the gist), the name of a ship or the name of a respectable organisation, such as the Admiralty.

However, ACAN provide strict guidelines for inappropriate names. You can't call it 'shit hill', 'plonker' promontory or 'cock mountain', unless of course your surname is Cock. You can't 'name it after a friend or someone you have a relationship with' – weird eh? You cannot name a peak after a 'sled dog or pet of any kind'. No Mount Fido then. And no names of companies or products are allowed; so there'll be no Virgin Summit then or Ford Mountain or Lego Ranges.

Thus fully equipped you proceed to Punta Arenas in Chile, charter a motor sailer and head for the Antarctic islands south of Elephant Island, where Shackleton almost came a cropper. Alexander Island, Thurston Island and Carney Island all have peaks waiting to be climbed and named. If you choose to land on the mainland, Ellesworth land with its Hudson Mountains is handy for picking up some first ascents. More seriously high is the Vinson Massif, which has many unclimbed mountains and peaks just waiting to be named. One other thing – it's cold.

61 Rocket scientist pick-up techniques

The late Professor Richard Feynman was a very clever man. Though he couldn't speak until he was three years old he quickly made up for it. At twenty-one he was the youngest person to work on the Los Alamos atom bomb project and won the Nobel Prize for discovering better ways of calculating quantum electrodynamics. He invented the concept of nanotechnology in his 1959 lecture 'There's plenty of room at the bottom'. He figured out why the space shuttle Challenger blew up and proved NASA wrong. He could play the bongos, paint and his textbooks have sold millions of copies. Strangely he only had an 'averagely high IQ' of 123, but then tests aren't everything.

Feynman was a scientist to his very core. When something didn't work he wanted to know why. And that included picking up women. He used to go regularly to a sleazy bar in New Mexico and though he chatted to lots of girls he never once scored ... and every time he ended up paying the bill. Finally a pair of friends – the MC who compèred the entertainment at the bar and his attractive wife – told him he had everything the wrong way round. They gave him three rules for success with women. These rules were based on the premise that women know that men want to appear a gentleman and not a tightwad. They exploit this to get what they want. When they are focused on getting what *they* want you never get what *you* want.

So Rule One is: disrespect women. Never be a gentleman. Rule Two: never pay for anything. Rule Three: never pay for anything unless they have agreed to go to bed with you *and you know they aren't lying*.

The friends added that it would work for all women, not just women in a bar seeking a good time.

As a scientist, Feynman felt duty bound to test these unlikely propositions. He spent the evening working himself up into a fervour of disrespectful thoughts aimed at women in general. Instead of projecting his usual considerate and likeable demeanour he focused on the show and didn't even glance at any lovelies who manoeuvred themselves into his line of vision. When one asked if she could sit next to him he muttered 'suit yourself'. The technique worked. He got into a conversation, bought no drinks and found himself walking the girl to her hotel. But then, in a moment of weakness, he bought her a coffee and a sandwich on the way. Suddenly she changed her tune and announced she'd got a date with someone else. Enraged, Feynman demanded the money back for her coffee. He returned to the bar disconsolate, but his friends congratulated him on being so tough. He thought he'd failed, but they told him to wait. Sure enough at 2 a.m. the woman popped her head back into the bar and told him to come up to her room.

Anxious to increase the statistical sample, Feynman attempted the trick on a girl he met at a dance at Cornell University. She was the sister of a fellow grad student. They went to the bar and ordered drinks and she waited for him to pay. Feynman said, 'Before I pay I just want to know will you sleep with me?'

'Yes.'

QED as the scientists say.

62 Survive in the desert even if terribly confused

Antoine de Saint-Exupery, author of the *Little Prince* and famed 1930s flyer, once crashed in the Sahara desert with only half a flask of coffee and an orange. The crash site was reportedly in Wadi Natrun, which is now on a major highway from Cairo to Alexandria. Back then it was far more remote, but still not more than 100km from a branch of the Nile. It was also midwinter, which makes a big difference in the desert as you need much less water. He and his mechanic Prevot successfully garnered two quarts of dew from stretched out parachutes, but spoiled it by storing it in an old fuel can. After walking around a lot by day and vacillating they headed east. Instead of heading towards the coast, or west, which is the way they believed Cairo lay, they walked east, 'because it felt right'. Just as Exupery and his companion were about to expire they were rescued by a lone Bedouin fortuitously in exactly the right place.

He was lucky. You should aim to be more prepared. For a start: take at least two oranges, if not twenty litres of water as an emergency back-up. Even in the hot summer, if you do nothing by day and walk by night, you can survive on three litres a day for seven days. You will be very dry, but you'll live. During the first Battle of Alamein, which was in August (the hottest time of year in the desert), the allied 'Desert Rats' were allowed five pints of water per day for cooking and drinking. That's about three litres. And they were active by day. You'll be hunkered down hopefully in the shade of some handy rock – even in the flattest part of the desert you'll usually find some kind of shade. If not, dig a shallow pit and arrange a tent or coat as a shade protector, but make the most of any cooling breezes of which there are thankfully a lot in the desert summer. To lie all day in the sun without shade is asking for death in two or three days.

If you are stranded in winter then the desert will be much cooler. By night you may even get a frost. You'll certainly need blankets and a warm hat. By day it may get up to the late twenties. So by adopting the night-walking or at least early-morning and evening-walking strategy you can get by on the same liquid as you would drink at home – a litre a day will suffice.

How far can you walk in a night? Sand walking is a killer, or can be. The sand causes blisters, both by getting into your socks and by making each step you take the same, and therefore rubbing the same spot without the variation you get when walking over pebbles and broken ground. The best footwear is sandals, but if you are wearing boots make sure you keep them clear of sand. If you are fearful of dying it is a great incentive. Without carrying a load, you should expect to manage 30km a night for seven nights: so you will, if fit and prepared, manage a 200km hike.

But what about carrying the water? One of the great unsung pioneers of desert safety was General Popski, who managed to persuade Churchill to finance his private army during the Second World War. Whenever Popski travelled in the Sahara in his jeep he carried a simple trolley made of bicycle wheels. On this, if his car faltered, he could escape carrying over 80 litres of water and supplies. The desert is mostly flat and dunes can often be circumvented, so a trolley works very well. Eighty litres will last you comfortably for three weeks ...

Without your trolley you're down to carrying the water. Bear in mind that 20 litres weighs 20kg or 44lbs: that's heavy and it will make you sweat – thus losing more water. If you are fit you might expect to make 15–20km the first few nights and then more as the weight decreases.

Knowing which way to walk is almost the easiest part, as long as you know where you are. Saint-Exupery's big problem was that he didn't. Without a GPS it's hard, but you can get a fix on latitude by sticking a stick in the sand and measuring the angle between the end of the shadow and the stick's top at midday. It's also possible to measure your longitude if you have an accurate watch or a radio which gives a time signal. If you know the exact time the sun should rise in the nearest city, you can then work out how far you are by the difference.

Far better is to have a basic knowledge of the terrain and where you have come from. Far better if Saint-Exupery had known that the desert is rocky and hilly east of Cairo and quite unlike the Western Desert where he landed. Bear in mind what you will do if there is an accident. The desert is not a labyrinth of paths waiting to snare and confuse you. It is more like a giant sea and the direction, once you know roughly where you are, is usually obvious. Find north at night by looking for the great bear, lining the outer two stars on the edge of the 'saucepan' and then sighting up to the slightly dimmer pole star. You know it's the right one as it's the only star that doesn't move all night. Mark the direction in the sand and keep walking, checking every so often with the pole star. If you sight up using other stars recheck every twenty minutes with the pole star to allow for a change of position.

By day you can find due south at midday – when the sun is at its highest it is also pointing south. At sunrise and sunset you also have perfect indications of east and west. And most likely there will be no clouds sufficient to cover up the sun's movement.

Should you find yourself lost and in a sandstorm or dust storm your best bet is to sit it out while visibility is nil. They rarely last more than a few days and often at night calm down enough for you to glimpse the night sky and get a fix on the pole star.

Before setting off on any desert trip memorise the main features. Most deserts have huge escarpments and straight endless roads that border the wilderness. These are the things to aim for – features you cannot miss even if you are off by twenty degrees in your walking.

Light travels far at night: you can see the lights of a medium-sized town 100km away in the desert. As for attracting others, if you choose to stay put then burn a tyre – the column of black smoke can be seen 60km away and will always attract other desert travellers.

The usual advice is to stay with your vehicle. If you have told people where you are going and when you'll be back, stay with the car and burn the tyres. If no one knows where you are and you are confident, walk. Think about that half-flask of coffee and that orange.

63 Be a DIY explorer

Exploration need not be the province of the wealthy nitwit, the billionaire with a big balloon or the sponsored serf dragging a sledge emblazoned with a corporate logo. Times have changed and thanks to lots of things being cheaper, mainly due to much increased air travel over the last twenty years, the era of the DIY explorer has finally come of age.

The original DIY explorer was Bill Tillman, a man who very nearly climbed Everest before the war and who after the war made many long journeys by sailing boat to remote Antarctic and Arctic islands. Once there he would explore, primarily the mountains, and made many first ascents along the way. With Eric Shipton he made the first crossing of the Patagonian ice

cap – a trip that is still a daring and difficult challenge. Tillman
fed his team on porridge and sardines mainly: the two great
staples of any DIY explorer – cheap, nutritious and a test of
character each time you face them.

The modern DIY explorer is faced with a shrinking world,
but not an utterly shrunken one. There are still vast tracts of
South America, New Guinea and Siberia that have neither
been properly mapped nor properly explored. Exploration is
one of those elastic concepts: you can explore a stretch of
stream in Herefordshire and that counts as exploration, albeit
micro-exploration. You can visit a place and explore the
people, notice something new about them or something that
reminds us about something that has been forgotten, and
that's also an aspect of exploring. After all, many of the early
African explorers were following information written by
Herodotus.

Decide on your destination: ice, jungle, desert, mountain,
swamp or steppe? Jungles are good and cheap and with
persistence good work can be done in Indonesia and
Venezuela particularly. In Venezuela, the *tepuis*, high buttes of
rock that rise thousands of feet out of the jungle and gave rise
to the Lost World idea of Conan Doyle, have not all been
climbed, let alone ascended. Even Roraima, the actual Lost
World, which features commercial trips each year, is only
visited along its side. The interior of the 25 square mile top is
still open to exploration.

The desert is also a good place to explore. Go by camel
having worked out the local rate rather than the tourist charge
and advertise for a rich companion to keep costs down. The
best way to start is to read old accounts by nineteenth- and
twentieth-century explorers and aim to follow their routes
until you get to spots where they announce they saw
something but had to press on. This is your jumping-off point

to explore properly. Using this method recent discoveries have been made near to Macchu Pichu, which were noted in passing by Hiram Bingham, but incredibly not followed up until nearly a hundred years later.

Gear should be bought most cheaply – preferably second-hand. *Loot* and other newspaper classified ads are good for rubber Avon-type boats and for outboard motors; eBay is excellent for hard-to-get items such as old maps and geographical journals. Half of exploration is about doing the right research: once you're halfway to the South Pole it's too late to hit the books, though with a satellite phone linked to a laptop you can always check something up on wikipedia.

The lure of hi-technology is best ignored, though. I've seen laptops waterlogged, video cameras misted up, sound recorders submerged – if it can get wet it will. Only with the greatest of care can delicate kit be kept from destruction. In the desert all cameras should be kept in two plastic bags, otherwise dust and sand will find a way in. In the jungle a video camera needs to be in a pellicase, which in turn should be in a seal-line-type waterproof sack. Whatever manufacturers say, neither pellicases (waterproof hard plastic suitcases beloved of film crews) nor seal-line bags (rolltop sealable plastic kit bags) are 100 per cent waterproof.

In the rain stick with 100 per cent waterproof plastic or coated nylon. Newfoundland long-line fishermen don't wear Gore-Tex, they wear rainproof gear that is solid plastic with poppers not zips which costs less than £100 for a complete outfit. And they *live* in the rain.

Using some kind of indigenous craft is a good way to see old country afresh. This is the kind of exploration that saw Thor Heyerdahl float across the Pacific on the 'Kon-Tiki' raft and Tim Severin the Atlantic in his leather craft 'Brendan'. Cheap indigenous craft include reed boats on the Blue Nile, inflated yak bladders on the Oxus, leather coracle-type craft in Tibet, basket-weave boats in southern India, not to mention Baidarka, or three-seat kayaks, in Siberia together with Umiak, skin boats in Greenland. Use one of these and you will perceive the world in a way quite different from the raft guide in shades navigating his super-safe inflatable. And indigenous craft bring out indigenous people. Taking a birch-bark canoe through Canada I met all manner of Indians who would normally have shunned another tourist in the outback.

For flights plan ahead and look for Internet bargains. Forget sponsorship: it takes too long and every sponsor tries to get their pound of flesh. If the place you need to get to is expensive to reach use lateral thinking to get there: we delivered a truck across Canada as a way of saving thousands in shipping costs for a ton of gear and a big canoe.

Last but not least travel with people who are enthusiastic, not accident-prone and who have a sense of humour. With these three you can go anywhere: I've taken people into serious wilderness for several months and their previous experience was a Cub camp for a week – and they were fine. Without humour and enthusiasm even the most experienced expert is more of a handicap than a benefit.

64 Crack a safe

Safe-cracking is on the decline. Violent crime is on the increase, or so it seems. Even criminals won't put the hours in these days: the easy pickings of a Securicor van robbed at gunpoint beats hours with the stethoscope and dial gauge cracking a safe.

To do this you listen to the levers through the stethoscope and when you hear the scraping noise of tumbler against lever you record it on the dial gauge to try and build up a map of the eccentricity of the tumbler. Eventually you decode your findings to crack the combination.

In all fairness to the crims, safes have got a lot harder to crack recently. The old standby of drilling in the right spot so that a screwdriver could be used to release the mechanism is far from easy anymore. Safes now feature layers of washers or ballbearings between the steel so any drill just spins. Embedded mild steel in concrete also wears out a drill bit. The thermal lance – a favourite Christmas present for every hard-core robber – is a dead loss on many modern safes as the heat results in burning up the contents.

Richard Feynman, that polymathic physicist, was adept at safe-cracking as we saw earlier. He discovered that even if you were one or two numbers wrong either side of the real number the safe still opened. That drastically reduced the number of combinations on a three-number safe from 1,000,000 to 8,000. At 400 combinations every half hour a safe usually gave up its secrets after four hours. There are several electronic 'crackers' that use this idea. Clamped to the front of the safe they work through this reduced number of combinations and are handily available on the Internet if you need one.

Feynman found that many people are simply too busy or lazy to even change the default combination on a new safe, usually 100–50–100. He also found that among scientists popular numbers were often used such as pi or the Boltzman constant. Less numerate folk mainly chose their birth date. Nowadays a would-be safecracker should also discover the victim's PIN number, another favourite choice for a combination.

For more serious cracking you need to enter the realm of drilling and listening, or more likely drilling and using a fibre-optic endoscope, to observe the inner workings of the bolt. A safe lock operates bolts that lock every side of the door. You need to activate the central mechanism to release those multiple bolts. The good news is that every safe manufacturer leaves a gap through which one can drill just in case they have to crack one of their own safes. Finding that Achilles heel, that spot under which there is only steel and not a drill-proof barrier, requires either luck, lots of test drills or a copy of the safe's plans. Or a diamond-core drill. In the last ten years diamond-core drills have given a new lease of life to safe-cracking. They go through everything. Only now are manufacturers experimenting with moving plates of mild steel which clog the drill up. Older safes are vulnerable though.

Once you are through (and this could be achieved by drilling through the back or side and feeding the endoscope around the corner), you can observe the back of the dial and see where the tumblers lie.

A method that takes a while but is seldom bettered is to place the safe in an acid bath – not too deep – and watch the base being eaten away. It's a lot more controllable than Semtex though it could take days. Another chemical trick is to immerse the safe in liquid nitrogen and then set about it with sledgehammers.

---

65 Build an emergency raft or boat

Emergency craft have a great appeal: who knows when one might need one to escape from rising floodwaters now that global warming is in the climatic driving seat.

The simplest emergency boats are made from found objects: pallets with plastic drums strapped to their underside, a duvet cover stuffed with bubble wrap, old inner tubes.

More interesting is to make a craft from natural materials. Logs are the most obvious, but beware: some, such as heart oak, actually sink, and others barely support any weight at all.

Twelve logs of larch each 30lb in weight – making a monstrously heavy 360lb raft – will only support a single 160lb man without sinking. Poplar is best (apart from super light woods like balsa): a 250lb raft will support 160lb in weight.

Reed rafts work much better: you can fashion a wooden frame and then bundle reeds beneath it to make it float. You can also inflate animal skins or, for the squeamish, plastic kit bags sealed tight with cord. These can be fastened under your raft frame.

Many travellers now carry inflatable thermorest mattresses. Four of these bound to a light wood frame will work as an inflatable to carry one man to freedom – say across a river swollen by seasonal rain. Chris McCandless, the subject of John Krakauer's book *Into the Wild*, died in the Alaskan wilderness because he dared not cross a river in flood. Even though he successfully killed a moose he made no move to use its skin as the covering for an improvised boat or as a float. The technique requires sewing up the skin as tightly as possibly around a stuffing of hay and thin branches. As inflated goatskins are commonly used as rafts on the Tigris, it is by no means farfetched to suggest this might have saved him.

Bamboo, if you are in tropical climes, makes for excellent raft material. Each sub-section within a pole is a self-contained flotation chamber. You can use long slivers of bamboo cut from the poles to tie the raft together.

If you have no saw or axe then you must burn down trees. Two men can start twenty small fires and attend to them all in order to fell twenty trees. For obvious reasons this method of felling has its vocal opponents, but if they are around then they can save you and you don't need a raft.

Dugout canoes are common from Canada to Chile. They are easy to make, but take time. The best tool is an adze. Start a fire on land and transfer the glowing coals to the log. Surround the embers with wet mud to contain the spread of the fire. Now build up the fire. Every few hours shift it along and hack away at the charred wood. It is time-consuming but not unpleasant work.

If you find yourself in gourd or calabash country, the Congo for example, these may be used as floats for a raft. Take the largest dried gourds you can find, line them upon two long thin logs and then tie two more logs along the top. The gourds thus trapped, you have a single long float. Make three of these, bind them together and you have a fine watercraft known locally as a *makara*.

If you can weave a basket shape large enough, you can cover it with the flysheet of your tent and make an excellent coracle. Willow is best for weaving, though any thin springy unseasoned wood will usually work.

Hide trays are used in both Peru and Tibet: take an ox hide and pinch up the corners, rather like pinching up the corners of a piece of paper to make a crude open box shape. Make holes at each corner top and use thongs to keep them together. Sticks can be wedged inside to give the 'tray' some solidity.

66 Trapping for townies

Trapping is neither pleasant nor easy work. Expect to meet
resistance both from concerned citizens and from your own
town-bred wimpishness. It's all very well telling yourself you're
covered by the merest veneer of civilisation, it's another thing
getting rid of it.

Trapping cannot, however, be learnt in an emergency. By
then it's far too late. You have to practise. As long as you eat
whatever you catch, trapping is no less humane than the
process that results in Big Macs and fish-fingers. Conscience
salved, move forward to the next stage of the primitive.

Trapping is, to paraphrase Lance Armstrong, not about the
trap. It's about the animal. A crap trap set right will win every
time over clever well-made traps in the wrong places that reek
of human scent. Indigenous tribes, who often leave much
trapping to the women and children, make do with some very
ropey looking contraptions – but they work. As a young
would-be trapper I spent hours and hours making traps that
always failed.

At that time I was concentrating on the simplest of traps:
the wire rabbit snare. My grandfather was an expert at
snaring. During the war, when meat was scarce, he fed his
family on snared rabbits. He even made the snares: from any
old wire, though brass picture wire is the usual choice. His real
skill lay in knowing where to set them.

My first success came when a friend and I fixed snares on
every 'run' that went under a long barbed-wire fence in a
nearby field. We must have set twenty snares. We then waited
until evening when the great family of bunnies came out to
browse on the luscious meadow grass. Up from our hiding

places armed with sticks and shouting we drove the frightened rabbits to their death. Well, we caught three. So the first lesson of trapping: overdo the number of traps. Close down all the options.

The next thing is to think like a rabbit (or a deer or a wild pig) and try and view what route you'd take past an obstacle, since a good place for a trap is in a 'run' that goes round a fallen tree or through a gap in a hedge. Thinking rabbit is not the exercise in telepathy it might seem. You are an animal, and still retain your animal senses, albeit overlaid by a liking for fine chardonnay and the minimalist music of Steve Reich. Or maybe not. Anyway, the point I'm making is that rabbits are quite a lot like humans. They dislike the cold and the wet. They like an easy life. They tend to take short-cuts. They are creatures of habit, but they are easily spooked. Using these principles look at a series of runs and think, 'Which one would *I* take?' This is the start of good trapping.

You can hone your trapping skill by mass trapping along hedge and fence lines. Mark the 'runs' that bear the most fruit well. Despite one way being the death of his relatives, rabbits will continue to use it out of sheer bad habit. The snares themselves should be wire loops an inch or two off the ground. Set them out wearing gloves and keep them out of the house so that they do not reek too heavily of the ways of men. Visit traps often to avoid giving a free meal to larger game.

Fancier traps follow the same principles (put out a large number, think like and observe your prey) but they are more fun. Complex homemade traps, reminiscent of those elaborate Vietcong booby traps that always get the platoon member who has yet to utter a word, are deeply satisfying to construct. Some even work. It's worth experimenting using *in situ* whippy branches pulled back as a driving force for a spear set ready along a trail. The trigger is just a tripwire or vine, which, when disturbed, upsets two forked sticks resting against each other. This releases the branch and fires the spear.

The deadfall is another trap popular and effective for crushing small mice and other inoffensive rodents. Take a very heavy log or stone and support it in such a way that jerking lightly with a string will release the weight. Hide and wait until your prey appears to eat the nuts or whatever you have left as bait. You can also make a kind of 'hair trigger' for a deadfall by having the support stick very finely balanced. More success usually attends to a manned trap, though manning is a tedious activity at the best of times, except for those intent on seeing nature at her rawest.

Baiting traps, as mentioned, aids success. For birds one can scatter grass seeds on a regular basis and build up an addiction to easy food. A net with its corners weighted with stones can be enough to trap birds intent on dinner. The iceman, found frozen five thousand years later in an alpine glacier, was carrying a bird net. They are still used in Portugal and parts of Spain. Most simply you lay the net out on bushes attended by birds or on the ground if it has been baited. Once their feet and wings are caught the birds tend to flap themselves further into entrapment. Pop them whole into soups and stews.

---

67 The last word on hangovers

Hangovers can be terribly personal things. One man's bad head does not equal another's. Based on considerable experience and wide scientific reading I will try my best to disseminate all I know.

Firstly, the effect of any drug is rather mysterious even to hard science. All drugs suppress or enhance existing neurotransmitters and other brain chemicals that run our brains for us. To drink while having a gregarious pile of fun produces far smaller hangovers than drinking alone or with people you don't really like.

But a hangover should first be defined and dissected. In Japan the word for hangover, is *futsukaoii* – literally 'two days' illness'. The Japanese know that a real corker does take two days to recover from – and sake and shochu, favourite Japanese drinks, both give cracking head-splitters the day after.

So, to break the hangover down: there is the pain of the almost-bearable headache, type one, which is usually caused by dehydration. Headache type two is the crushing, ghastly feeling that some form of nuclear explosion has taken place without permission somewhere within your cranium. This is caused by the breakdown of impure methanol into purer ethanol before absorption by your system. There is sickness in the stomach, which may or may not be resolved by throwing up; there is what Evelyn Waugh described so well as 'feeling ninetyish'; there is the vacuous head stuffed up feeling that is bearable as long as you don't need to concentrate.

Getting rid of the stomach ache, the headache and the fragile 'ninetyish' feeling all constitutes a hangover cure.

Naturally you've forgotten to drink that litre of water before bedtime. If you did, and managed to pop a single aspirin or paracetamol, you'll probably wake up feeling fairly OK. But you didn't. If it's primarily a feeling of your stomach ailing then good old Alka-Seltzer is your best bet. If it makes you throw up then you'll feel better too. Sometimes seltzer can be 100 per cent effective in a few minutes – a true invention of genius.

If I've actually been forced to get up, my hangover cure breakfast is boiled eggs – two – plus a can of coke. Maybe coffee too, if you can manage it. Coca Cola was originally designed as a hangover cure and was sold as such in drugstores in the US before people got a liking for it as an ordinary drink. But it works very well in its original function. The yolk of boiled, or even raw, eggs contains chemicals that facilitate the breakdown of methanol into ethanol. Methanol is the dirty form of alcohol; purer forms have more ethanol – pure vodkas, for example, give far less nasty hangovers. Egg yolk gets rid of that methanol faster and cures your monstrous head problem. Hair of the dog also works because it tops up the alcohol in your system and smooths the transition from methanol to ethanol.

Pure oxygen inhaled from an emergency cylinder available from all good chemists is a wonderful cure. The pounding you have given your brain cells results in their oxygen starvation; hence walking and swimming as cures – by upping respiration they up the oxygen levels. Hemingway was a great believer in the morning swim as a hangover cure. However, there is often a deal of pain to go through before the oxygen starts piping through. Deep-breathing exercises are a more civilised version – Christopher Isherwood claimed that yoga deep-breathing exercises always cured his hangovers. I have also found that doing a series of fake Tai Chi or other Grasshopper-style martial arts moves in slow motion is good for aiding the dispersal of a crippling hangover – the worst kind when you can't even sleep.

The final advice which you won't take: start your drinking with a mineral water and alternate throughout the evening. Only drink when you eat. Sip wine very slowly and never gulp. Like I said, ignore it.

68 How to wield an axe

Most people are crap with axes, including myself until I undertook a diligent study of the art. It takes time and patience to learn. You need a sharp axe. Most of all you need to know that less often equals more when it comes to the use of an axe.

First, splitting. This is the only use of an axe widely practised these days. A saw is sensibly used to reduce a tree trunk to logs and then an axe is used to split that into useable chunks. A fat-bodied splitting axe works best, but almost any axe will do, even a blunt one.

But you need a sharp axe to chop trees down or to chop logs in two like a real lumberjack. Sharpen your axe with a metal file until all the dings are gone and the blade cuts wood without pressure.

The actual chop itself is done by the axe – not your shoulders. Indigenous people leave a lot of wood chopping to women and if you watch them at work you can learn a lot. Almost lazily they raise their machete or axe and then let it fall using its own weight only slightly accelerated. You can chop for hours like this.

With a long felling axe bring it high enough for you to feel in control (this will get higher as you get better) and just let it fall. When it's almost past you add your own force to the downward momentum, but don't strain yourself. Chop at a manageable rhythm. To aim for a spot just look at it and the axe will follow, a bit like teeing off in golf.

Here's the big axe secret: when people chop logs in two they start cutting a small 'V' and then they realise to make it deeper they have to make it wider and wider. So a lot of their chopping is just widening the hole – which is wasted effort.

To cut a log a foot in diameter you need to make a cut a foot wide. Start by making one axe chop on one side and another, at a slight angle a foot away. Then lever the axe sideways and split out the intervening wood. Magic! Instead of shaving away constantly at both sides you just took out a whole hunk of wood. Just keep repeating this double action as you go down through the log and each chop will naturally get closer and closer to the other. Get into a steady rhythm and you'll beat any muscled tyro who thinks it's all about chopping like a mad axeman.

To take down a tree with an axe employ the same principles but sideways on. First, however, chop out a section in the back of the tree lower down than you intend to cut at the front. This lower cut will be the direction the tree should fall (assuming it's not leaning). It only needs to be about a quarter of the way through the tree.

Then go around to the front and if the tree is two feet wide start chopping gashes about eighteen inches apart. Split out each chunk as before. If the tree starts to move you can give it a push in the right direction. Remember to shout 'Timber'!

69 Commit hara-kiri

There have been rumours emanating from the boardroom for weeks, but now it's confirmed. The company must slim down. Naturally you are a highly valued, long-serving and efficient team player – so it's your head on the block. The shame is too much. You have kids in private school. Your wife has an expensive show-jumping habit. The Japanese film you saw years ago gives you an idea: go out honourably by committing hara-kiri, or *seppuku* as the Japanese also call it.

You'll need a sharp knife, preferably with ten inches of blade. Macho survival online stores should provide the real thing – razor sharp, too. You'll need a mate who isn't afraid of going to prison for manslaughter – that could be hard; he's the one who will behead you with a katana, also available online for about £150. A katana is a Japanese sword.

There are various grades of hara-kiri. The most lightweight is simply to dig the knife into your stomach and make a small incision. The most drastic, called *jumonji*, is to cut laterally for about four inches at navel height, and then cut upwards allowing the intestines to fall through the stomach wall. That takes, or took, guts.

Then the *kaishaku*, or second, chops your head off with the sword. Even this isn't so simple, as novelist Yukio Mishima found when he committed *seppuku* in 1970. His first second made three attempts and it took a second faithful disciple to sever his head. Later reports tell that Mishima managed a very deep but not very long cut across his stomach. The knife went in over four inches. Oral transmissions in traditional fencing schools advise a cut no deeper than two inches, as any deeper causes an involuntary movement pitching you forward. This indeed happened to Mishima, which is why the first attempt to cut off his head ended in the blade hitting the top of his shoulders.

Before you demand your second to take your head off you are supposed to write a death poem in your own blood. If you fear that inspiration may desert you as your stomach flops onto the tatami, you are allowed to compose one earlier and simply sign it with a bloody squiggle.

The clothes you wear are important, too. A short white jacket open at the belly and a kind of wound skirt called a *hakama*, also white, is the traditional costume. White, of course, shows up the blood better.

But, on second thoughts, don't do it. Pour yourself a dry Martini instead.

70 Hedgehoggery

Hedgehogs are a pest aren't they? You're playing footie in the garden and manage a nice swerving corner when, bang, you've punctured the ball on good old Mr Hedgepig trundling across the lawn. Though kids like hedgehogs, it's well known they harbour ticks and other nasties inimical to the ultra-clean environments we all prefer these days. Yes, it's time to get rid of that hedgehog once and for all.

This is an old gypsy trick. Lure the hedgehog out of the bushes with a bowl of milk (which actually they cannot digest even though they like to drink it – water is better if you are a hedgepig lover, which you aren't). Grab the hedgehog in a pair of stout gardening gloves. He will roll into his tiresome protective ball. Now liberally coat him with a two-inch thick layer of sticky clay. Pop him into the embers of a large bonfire and cook for an hour.

This method of cooking removes all the spines leaving edible and flavoursome hedgehog for all to share.

71 Whittling a woggle

Hitler was a whittler. His favourite outdoor pastime, at least in the early stages of the war, was whittling. Apparently he was quite good at carving small ducks and woodland birds. If that hasn't put you off, read on.

Whittling is taken seriously in Scandinavian countries. You can buy special whittling knives and even join whittling clubs – some mixed, some single sex and by invitation only. For a beginner only the barest minimum of equipment is required. That is one of the attractions of whittling: its stripped-down and utterly unpretentious nature.

A good knife that is sharper or as sharp as a razor is essential. Many a whittler has lost part of thumb or forefinger not through an excess of sharpness but its opposite. A blunt knife encourages the use of brute force to make the blade cut. This excess more often than not causes the blade to jump and bury itself in the softest object to hand – which is usually *your* hand.

Refer to earlier sections on sharpening to get your blade super sharp. A good whittling knife can be bought for very little from the back pages of any gun magazine. Go for a curly birch-handled Swedish design with a simple blade of about five inches long. Most are stainless steel, but carbon steel is easier to get a good edge on. Alternatively, use a Stanley-type knife with disposable blades. It's not as good, or as satisfying, but it works. A small chisel can come in handy for digging out difficult bits.

With your super sharp knife it's time to whittle on. A stick is a good first subject. Walking sticks are always welcome gifts and are not hard to whittle. Select a piece of hazel for your first stick as it won't require any straightening. When you become proficient any old bent bit of wood will do, as your first task is to straighten it by immersion in a rainwater barrel and then holding it over a fire hot enough to draw steam from the wood. Then drill a large hole in the seat of an old wooden stool or chair and use this as a grip in order to bend the stick straight. Even wobbly lengths of thorn can be straightened this way.

With your straight hazel decide on the type of stick you'd prefer. A thumb stick is easy: simply lop off the branch at a natural fork and incorporate this into the handle. Strip off all the bark and leave for a day or two to dry. That's all the seasoning a stick needs. Rules about seasoning stem from high-class cabinet making where complex furniture is expected to be kept under dry and warm conditions. Your stick is simple and can be best fashioned 'green'.

Trim the stick until it's smooth all over. Use a short piece of copper tube to make a ferrule and the stick is ready. Whittle in your initials and any heraldic devices that take your fancy.

A more difficult stick with a curved handle can be made by steaming a right-angle bend at one end. If you want a shepherd's crook get hold of a curly sheep's horn either by finding a dead sheep in the hills or from a craft company. Sand the horn down and coat with varnish. Cut a long, tapering tang at the point you wish it to join the stick. Cut a matching elongated 'V' for it to fit into. Glue it in place with araldite and then bind it tightly with whipping thread from a chandlers. Alternatively drill both the handle and the stick and use a self-tapping length of bolt to hold both parts together (having lopped the head off the bolt once it is securely screwed in at one end).

151

Having mastered sticks you can move on to wooden cups and spoons. A great help in spoon and cup making is a curved knife known as a crook or crooked knife. Alternatively you can use a scorb, which is a kind of sharp scooping knife. Lacking either of these you can use a chisel and knife combination, though it is more laborious. Sycamore makes for good spoons and cups as it is odourless. To make a cup with a handle cut off a length of trunk of a small tree for the body and keep attached a short twig to be whittled into the handle.

Whittling a woggle is something to warm the heart of any ex-Boy Scout. A woggle is the ring device used for securing the two ends of a neckerchief around your neck. Wooden woggles with elaborate carving are highly prized. Get a piece of hardwood and whittle it down into a 3cm diameter wood cylinder about 3cm deep. Either drill or use a hot poker to remove a good portion from the centre to make a crude hole. Enlarge the hole with careful knife-work. Engrave your old patrol animal or any beast with which you feel some shamanic or otherwise connection on the rim of the woggle.

Carving animals in relief as a form of decoration for sticks, woggles and cups looks hard but isn't much harder than drawing. Indeed for a difficult animal trace a simplified outline onto the wood. Use your sharpest knife to cut around it. For tips, go into a church with old carving, and see how they do it. The key for this kind of detail work is the razor sharpness of a knife so that it can cut across the endgrain like butter.

More elaborate whittling projects may suggest themselves. A man in America recently whittled a car. That's right, he spent five years whittling away to make a wooden body shell to sit on a wooden chassis he also whittled. Only the wheels, engine and steering were made of metal.

Some whittlers like to go microscopic and whittle things from matchsticks. For this you need a big magnifying glass of

the kind used by fly tyers and a couple of surgical scalpels.
A great test piece for micro-whittlers is to carve several
interconnecting links of a chain from a single match. Don't
accidentally strike the match head, though, or you could
watch months of work go up in flames.

72 Exotic treehouses

A treehouse, like a boat, is a symbol of freedom. Usually cheap
or even free to build, and without any territorial claim, it sits
high in the sky reminding us of our ancestral origin in the
branches. Building a treehouse fit for an adult is not so very
different to those cobbled-together dwellings you may have
built as a child. But now you have more money and better
skills, so the result can only be better.

First off, forget drawing plans or anything boring like that.
At most make a few rough sketches of how it *might* look. I have
found that materials, and the base tree, affect what you can
build to such an extent that it's best to be really flexible. That
said, it's a lot easier if the floor is flat and the walls upright.

What kind of tree or trees you use is usually down to what's
available. If you have three ashes in a group you can nail
planks between them to construct a basic triangular house.
You can then extend the base timbers out front to make a kind
of prow or balcony. Balconies or verandahs are essential for
adult treehouses as this is where you sit and sip your gin and
tonic as the sun goes down over your neighbours' gardens. In
early morn the balcony also makes a good sniping platform for
eliminating by air rifle any persistent pigeons, squirrels or
other pests.

Nail into the trunk. Though the tree will probably be screaming with pain, it will be hopefully at any inaudible frequency. Big fat trees don't die from having a few six-inch nails knocked into them, think of it as like having your leg pinned after a nasty accident. If you are too civic-minded to nail your host tree, then build a wooden girdle resting on sack cloth to protect the bark. This can also be supported by wooden pilings that rest on the ground.

However you decide to support the base timbers you'll need to nail a floor to them to make the initial platform. All this wood can come from B&Q, but it's much cheaper to use old pallets, wood from skips and used wood from scrapyards. Old wood seems to suit treehouses better. And lest you think treehouses are of little consequence, Alnwick Castle, the model for the *Harry Potter* films, has recently paid £7million to build an entire restaurant up in the trees.

Anyway, your own treehouse can be very high or quite close to the ground. A very high tree, such as Douglas Fir or Scotts pine, with suitably tethered ladders running up it can make a very impressive treehouse. The ladders are best roped and bolted into position to allow for any movement – and there will be quite a lot a hundred feet up. The same principles apply for building the base platform – nail a ring of short 2×4s around the trunk using a spirit level to keep them all flat. At a point some four feet higher nail two long cross pieces either side of the trunk extending say five feet each way. Now make a triangle from these beams down to the lower supporting ring. Repeat with beams going at right angles. You now have an eight-sided shape braced against the trunk a hundred feet off the ground. Lay a floor across the beams and then build walls and add windows and a roof. The roof can be made as a reverse of the floor with an eight-sided pattern of beams sticking out from the trunk, but braced from above this time.

Windows can be installed readymade – any old ones can be nailed in place and then the walls around them adjusted to fit. The roof is simplest covered in shed roofing felt. You could also use corrugated plastic or even several sheets of polythene, though that really will make it look like part of an eco-protest.

A trapdoor is essential in any treehouse – if only to keep kids out. Fashion one by simply cutting a hole in the floor and adding hinges and a securing bolt. Feed the last section of the ladder up through the hole, but cut two recesses so you can shut the door without removing it.

Treehouses of a very exotic and deluxe nature can be fitted

with fridges. Get hold of a twelve-volt camping fridge and a car battery. Wire the battery to as many cheapo Motorola solar panels as you can afford. Fix the panels to the roof. Another source of power is to fix a small windmill and generator out on a pole some distance from the treehouse. For the less self-sufficient, run a power line from the house down the tree trunk and then overhead and indoors (don't bury a power line unless it's armoured as, sooner or later, you'll go over it with a mower or hit it with a spade).

For some reason treehouses look good adorned with flags. Design your own which can be raised when you are in residence. Spend nights sleeping in your treehouse feeling the sway of the wind like being at sea.

---

73 Growing giant vegetables

Giant vegetables are a sure sign of machismo at some elemental level. It's fun, too, to produce grotesque marrows and spuds the size of rugby balls. Beware, though, the flavour of giant veg is weak and bland – small is better when it comes to taste.

First off for a giant cabbage and onion man is to sort your seeds, then it's all manure and water. Big babies give birth to giants when fully grown. Find the seeds that are famous for hugeness through diligent Internet research. The current world record for giant carrots is the aptly named 'Jumbo' variety. To grow one to compete get a four foot by six inch plastic drainpipe and fill it with sand. Use a broom handle to rod out a hole which you should fill with the richest peaty compost you can make or buy. Plant three jumbos and weed out the weakest after they've germinated. Water regularly from the top for the first two months and then from beneath so that the roots seek out moisture. Guard against pests. Hose out the sand at harvest time and claim your whopping carrot.

The giant vegetables of Findhorn in Scotland were all grown in very sandy soil very close to the beach and with masses of horse manure. They were well tended – vegetables, like people, love attention.

Giant potatoes are not that huge – typically around the 7lb mark. Grow them in mounds of sand with manure well dug in. When the potatoes are small reach through the soil and remove the smaller ones with great care so that all the growing effort goes into the biggest of the bunch.

Giant pumpkins are among the biggest of giant things you can grow. The current world record is held by Joe Jutras of Rhode Island with a pumpkin the size of a car weighing 1,689lb. Pumpkins weighing 1,000lb are within the reach of the keen amateur as long as you attend to them carefully. Use Dill's Atlantic Giant seeds and plant early in a heated cold frame in a good mound of well-composted soil. Use liquid fertiliser to get maximum early growth. Keep piling earth in a mound over the tap root even after you remove the cold frame. Hand-pollinate the flowers at an early stage of the season using a camel-hair brush to dust the pollen onto the stamens. Pull off all the flowers except the most promising. When pumpkins appear remove all of them except two. When one seems to be the best, keep only that one. Water and fertilise like crazy. You can almost never give a pumpkin too much water. Carve your giant pumpkin into a carriage, add wheels and go to the ball.

74 Brew up tea like a Desert Rat

The Desert Rats of the British Eighth Army could not fight
without their tea. Or they could, but tea definitely helped.
Unlike the Germans, whose brew-ups required petrol stoves
and ersatz coffee, the hardy rats only needed a handful of
leaves and a couple of petrol tins.

The Germans, in their quest for efficiency, had designed an
unbeatable petrol can; the 'jerry' can used today the world
over and unchanged in sixty years. The Allies had to make do
with flimsy four-gallon petrol tins, a third of which leaked. It
has been estimated that the initial early losses by the British in
North Africa were down to the incredible fuel losses from
these fragile tins.

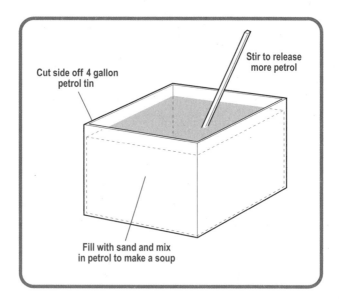

Stir to release
more petrol

Cut side off 4 gallon
petrol tin

Fill with sand and mix
in petrol to make a soup

But the tins had some advantages when it came to brewing up. Cut the side out of one, lie it lengthways on the ground, half fill it with sand and then add petrol until you have a very thick soupy mix. Light it. Against all expectation of exploding fuel you'll find it burns with a controllable blue/yellow flame for ages. The sand acts as a damper to the volatility of the petrol. When the fire begins to falter just stir the soup and it will revive again. Another tin, cut down and held over the flames to burn off any residual petrol taste, serves as a kettle. Fill with water, chuck in the tea leaves and sugar and wait for a perfect brew.

---

75 Grow your own painkillers

Naturally, the only need one might have for opium is during a potential emergency, something like the movie *The Eighth Day*, when all government services have collapsed or are unable to reach you. In such a situation with many casualties you will need to know how to manufacture your own painkillers.

Order your seeds now: *papaver somniferum* are the ones to ask for – purple poppies, you see them in garden centres quite often. They're not illegal and can be stored for three to five years, so you can stockpile them against the possible collapse of society as we know it.

Once you have ample evidence that painkillers are no longer available, plant your seeds. In the UK you can plant in late December or early spring. Tend them carefully for the first few months – poppies are most at risk in the early stages. Make sure you plant a lot as some will fail, though the English climate, with its cool evenings and warmer days, is fine for poppy growing. You may even drive by fields of purple poppies in the Home Counties where they are grown for commercial morphine production. Or were – before the apocalypse we are now projecting.

In early summer you should have a nice patch of purple. Wait for the petals to fall and then watch the grey band around the top of the seed pod get darker and darker. When it is almost black the opium is ready to harvest.

Using a sharp blade, maybe your whittling knife, make an incision no deeper than a millimetre or two all round the seed-pod. Watch the white opium bubble out. Leave it for three to six hours whereupon it will be crusty and brownish. Scrape it off and store it. A few days later you can repeat this with another incision a little lower. You can harvest the same pod up to three or four times if you're lucky. Smoking in a pipe is the usual method of administering it as a painkiller and the easiest if syringes and other medical supplies are unavailable. Remember if you harvest your opium while there is still a civil government in Britain, you may have some explaining to do.

76 Eating skunk, sloth, civet cat, slug, snail, termites, rat and swan

Skunks cannot only be eaten, they also make good pets when properly deodorised. Take your skunk to the vet and have the scent gland removed under a local anaesthetic – it's quick and painless apparently. Skunks are intelligent and loyal and love being cuddled by kids. They can eat almost anything from yoghurt to old vegetable scraps though they do need a clean bowl of water to drink from.

Should your interest in skunks take a more sinister turn

then they are also highly recommended for the table. Skin the skunk and gut it. Then roast and serve with cranberries – according to William Byrd, writing in the eighteenth century, skunk 'is surprisingly sweet'.

Sloths make easy game as they move so slowly. You can choose from either the two-toed or three-toed varieties. Gastronomically there is little difference. Both are vegetarians and sensibly stay out of sight mostly in high trees. South American Indians knock them out of the branches with stones or poison darts loaded with curare. The creature is usually roasted over a fire with little ceremony, though sloth stew, cooked slowly with wild garlic and turmeric is reportedly a real jungle delicacy.

Civet cat can be found in many jungles, but I have eaten this on numerous occasions and it is not good. Whether as a stew, roasted or fried, it always has a nasty musky flavour. Only consume if desperate. However, the Chinese rate it as a delicacy. A famous Chinese dish called 'dragon and lion' pairs civet cat with peacock flesh.

Snails are eaten by the French we know, but beyond that most people are a little hazy on the details. There are huge deposits of edible snail shells in the Pyrenees left over from Stone Age times, so apparently the French have always loved them. The escargot they most favour are the Roman land snails *Helix pomatia* and *Helix aspersa*. These should be kept in special snail gardens called cochlearia to make sure they don't consume anything foul. Snails tend to taste of what they eat. Keep them supplied with fine lettuce and fatten them on milk. To cook a snail kill it by boiling, stuff it with a mix of garlic and chopped chestnuts and then roast in a low oven.

In Africa slugs are also eaten, but when one dropped in a cup of tea I was drinking it gave to the brew such a foul taste it put me off them for ever. Theoretically they are edible, but the slime they are encased in must be scrubbed or boiled off assiduously.

Termites are a favourite Bantu dish. The recipe is:

One pint of termites
One teaspoon of ground palm nut oil
Salt to taste

Remove termite wings and dry the termite on a hot stone in the sun. Smear a pan with oil and fry them up until crisp. Salt them and eat like popcorn. Keep some as they remain edible for months.

Rats are edible if fed on grain. The Chinese have seventeen ways of preparing them, including the delicious Golden Rat of Canton. Thoreau claimed he ate rat on Walden Pond, skinned, gutted and fried with a little relish. G. Gordon Liddy, the Watergate burglar, also claimed he ate rat 'fried the American way', though this could have been an obscure allusion to his preferred method of dealing with traitors.

Swan. There are too many swans in England and eating them may not be a bad idea, though it could put you on death row. My grandfather once killed and ate a mute swan, which is still a treasonable offence and therefore theoretically punishable by death – as is sabotage in a naval dockyard (the death sentence was famously removed from UK statute books, but only for murder). Being a lucky scamp my granddad seems to have gotten away with it.

There are seven species of swan and only the mute, *Cygnus olor*, is Crown property. The only other people allowed to own mute swans are the two ancient livery companies of London – the Vintners and the Dyers. A mute swan with two nicks in the side of its beak belongs to the Vintners, one nick means the Dyers. All other mutes are the property of Her Majesty.

If you come across a black swan from Tasmania you can grab it for the pot. Other white swans up for grabs are the

Bewick's and whooper swans. You can tell them from mute swans as they tend to be smaller with a black dot of an eye rather than an eye enlarged by the mascara effect of black colouring that mute swans have. Mute swans, despite their name, are not silent. They can snort and hiss and make an explosive 'heoor' sound.

A swan can give a nasty peck on the backside, but its wings cannot break an arm or a leg, despite the rural myth. Those with goose expertise will know best how to grab and kill them, though it will not be a doddle for a first timer. Twisting a bird's neck is easier said than done. With someone to hold the bird down to a butcher's block the quickest and most humane way is to chop the head off with a machete. Then pluck and draw it and cook like a goose or a large duck.

77 Shedhead

Men love sheds. Sheds speak to them of freedom and calm. Often, it's the nearest they get to the wide and wild outdoors. A shed can be the purest expression of a man's innermost desires, or it can be a right pigsty – and it doesn't matter, which is part of the beauty of sheds. No one tells you to 'clean that shed up we've got visitors coming'. Kids aren't allowed in: 'Touch that lawnmower, router, hedge trimmer, circular saw, box of Silk Cut and you could be killed.' The heavy aura of masculine pastimes protects the shed from intruders of the wrong kind. A shed can be booby trapped and no one would have any sympathy for the victim. Sheds can be *dangerous*.

Sheds may be the last hope for the endangered male who fears for his masculinity now that oestrogen is in the water supply, beef steak and even smoked salmon. A shed could make a good tomb, if hung with the right inscription and perhaps a continuous flaming torch such as the ones you sometimes get outside fancy restaurants.

Let there be no jesting when it comes to sheds. Sheds run deep and perforce silent. To women they are places of amusement if not downright mockery. Young men have no need of sheds as domestic battles are still on the horizon. With the inevitable losses, like a wounded Napoleon all men turn to their shed as a last-ditch stand against something they only obscurely know is against their innermost nature.

OK – to business. A shed is most certainly not to be taken as lightly as, for example, a treehouse might be. Oh no. A shed is men's business, as dark and mysterious as any Aborigine Turinga board. To buy a readymade shed is OK. Better to inherit one that is unique in some way. Even better to build one: your very own dream shed.

Don't be in a rush. My shed took six months to build, a six months dogged by ironic jeering as I had told my wife it would be up 'in a couple of weekends'. But as soon as I laid out the foundations for my shed I was gripped by the absolute conviction I should do everything *as well as possible*. I knew I would be judged by other shedheads on the craftsmanship of my shed. But it wasn't just that, I felt that building my shed demanded a commitment to excellence bordering on the mystical, the kind of commitment I most definitely didn't have to putting up IKEA shelves and replacing light fittings. With the foundations and uprights raised I sat in the skeletal interior of my shed with a glass of wine and a small cigar. I could view the heavens through the star-shaped roof beams. A great and welcome calm came over me.

Work proceeded at a snail's pace. Often I just needed to walk round the shed staring for a long time at different parts.

Sometimes this was to solve a problem (and there were many as my shed was octagonal in shape), but other times it was a kind of psychic catching of my breath. I gave up using power tools as I found any time saved I just used up in staring at joists and floorboards. I found that hand tools are fine for almost any job; they build strength and muscle too, the stringy hard muscle that you can't get in the gym.

My shed had a pointed roof reminiscent of some of the excesses of Ludwig II of Bavaria. When I overheard a shedless neighbour comment to his wife that mine was a 'shed on steroids', I was absurdly pleased. Indeed the excessive height of my shed's roof and ceiling gave being inside it a cathedral freedom to exhale and be at one with the present moment.

Enough of my own shedquest: each man must follow his own path to the bottom of the garden. Suffice it to say, I can pass on a few pointers for those eager to join the tribe of shed.

If you buy a bought shed get the absolute biggest you can afford. No shed is ever big enough. Customise it, too – put an extra door in and even a storage cellar beneath. Cut a trapdoor in the floor and just dig down into the earth below. You don't need to cement it – just make sure that when it rains the water is collected and doesn't seep under your shed. You can install lengths of pottery pipe in the cellar to store wine at exactly the right temperature.

Strangely I found the less I cut corners the more I got into shed building and the more I enjoyed it. It was as if the shed was teaching me to take pains, be expansive, refuse to take second best, abjure for ever the rush and tear of modern life. A simple square design I found boring, but the moment I sketched my fantasy eight-sided übershed I was filled with a massive surge of creative energy.

Interior décor of the shed: of course it's up to you, but I found that plain wood did just fine. I think any shed looks good with diagrams and old photographs in frames hanging between the cobwebs. Maps never go amiss. I also made one of those racks to hang every single tool on, though I stopped short of drawing a white outline around it.

Sheds can be used to store both books and machines with an oily smell like a chainsaw or an outboard. Damp in sheds can be a problem: one I solved with a timer plug and one of those cheap electrical oil radiators. Power was simply an ultra-long extension cord from the house that ran along the top of the fence – as with treehouses, avoid burying anything except a proper armoured cable. When it got very, very cold and I was working away at my laptop, I would drape a big tablecloth over my desk and put my legs and the radiator underneath it. This was always as warm as toast.

Shed windows are easily made: just buy the glass in sheets and saw lengths of wood to fit around them. One of the problems with readymade sheds is the size and height of the windows – they are often too small and too low. Especially in those ghastly summerhouse-type constructions, which are really Wendy houses and can only be revived by housing a collection of antique fowling pieces. Big, high windows are great – low enough to see out of when standing and too high for kids and neighbours to see in.

Inviting friends round to your shed is quite fun and unusual, as most men, like the last of the mastodons in the frozen north, have retreated into lonely individuality, with their shed a last and lonesome outpost. It is true that a shed is closer to a hermit's cave than it is a pub, but that doesn't have to be the case. Install a small wood-burning stove and a few leather armchairs of the very comfy variety. Get friends round, pour out the Bowmore and play a few hands of poker. Shed conversations can be enlivened by shooting with BB guns at pictures of well-known and reviled politicians. Have an 'ideas session' – brainstorming in sheds produces quite different ideas to brainstorming in offices. Often you may exit the shed and yet be unwilling to return to the cleanliness and prissiness of the house. Light a fire round the back – impromptu barbecues and sheds go well together. Sheds make a good base for bonfire night, too.

---

78 Perfect flying in economy class

Economy is cramped, loo starved and, if the airline is European or American, staffed by unattractive men and women who are deaf and stupid. First tip: fly Third World. Zambia's national airline is superb – they send the drinks trolley round every half hour; Egypt's is pretty good; and Air India is the only airline I know where an elderly gent was allowed to stay in the recline position during landing because he was asleep.

But let us say you're unlucky and stuck on a BA flight with a stewardess whose main aim in life is to get her job done as quickly as possible without reference to your desires or comforts or the fact that the bloody ticket cost £500.

First off, obviously get yourself an aisle seat: window seats are cramped and you're at the mercy of others when you want to go to the loo. Secondly, if choosing vegetarian as a way to avoid food poisoning, pre-check that airline's recipes. Some airlines do great vegetarian (BA, Lufthansa and Air India), but some are rubbish – Iberia being just one example.

Better food advice is to bring your own wholesome grub so that you can ignore the crap they have on offer. Chicken drumsticks, ham on rye, cheese and chutney sandwiches,

caviar, brie, champagne and Perrier water. Bring a flask –
empty through the X-ray – and have it filled with Costa coffee
before you board. Buy the newspapers and magazines you
want to read plus a couple of the latest bestsellers or other
piffle that catches your eye. The whole key is to be able to tune
out the airline staff who have, by training and experience, seen
you as a psychiatric nurse sees a mentally ill pensioner i.e.,
a dimwit who can't control his or her bladder. Kids are given
a little bit of leeway – but not a lot. Your best bet is to be
independent and not pathetically waiting for them to 'serve'
you. Turn off the blower above your head as soon as you can
or you'll catch a cold.

As for films: forget the cruddy unintelligible crackling you
get in their disposable earphones and bring your own laptop
with the films you want to see, downloaded or on DVD, which
you can watch wearing your own hi-fi earphones of the best
Dolby quality. Take off your shoes and wear plastic sandals so
you don't tread in other people's piss when you go to the loo.

Have a pen in your pocket to fill out the immigration card
and make sure you keep the seat stub in your passport for the
flight details and passport number. On leaving, brazenly swipe
the unclaimed first-class 'gifts' as presents for children.

79 Long-distance walking for pain and pleasure

The modern equivalent of the medieval pilgrimage is the long-
distance walk, often from Land's End to John o'Groats but
also round the coastline or up and down the Pennine Way.
Abroad there are the GR11 and GR10 (*grande randonnées*),
which span the Pyrenees, the GR20 around Corsica and the

Mackenzie Trail across British Columbia, to name but a tiny selection of jolly good hikes.

Long-distance walking calls to the inner masochist and to the crypto religious sentiment of *ambulans solvare* (Latin for 'walking solves everything'). Big hikes get you right away from people, litter, noise and cars. They are an excellent way to stay or get fit. They are extremely cheap. When you finish you have a permanent sense of achievement. What could be a better hobby?

A few nasty demons stand between you and successful completion of your first long-distance walk. Many are tempted to give up because they have refused to acknowledge these gremlins, these devils that seek to derail the modern pilgrim. The three worst are: blisters and other foot problems; rain; and poor nutrition. Any one of the above can cause such a devastating drop in morale that the long-distance attempt is shelved.

Feet are all about boots, well, boots and socks. The expensive nylon-lined walking socks that guarantee no blisters do not work, but they do help. Thick socks are always better than thin socks as they absorb more sweat. Sweat is what moistens your feet, makes them soft and therefore prone to blisters.

The second blister causer and potential Achilles tendon rubber is carrying a heavy rucksack after all your practice hiking was done with no load. An extra 15kg will squash your feet flatter and alter the way you walk sufficient to give you killer blisters.

Practice is the best cure. Refer to my blister section for more details (page 73).

Rain stops play – but it doesn't need to. When hiking in wet places like Britain you need to be prepared for a week of rain. Gaiters will keep your lower legs dry and a good poncho will protect you and your rucksack. I have cut overtrousers into 'overshorts' and used these to protect my thighs and knees – the advantage is that you reduce condensation. In any event overtrousers should be baggy.

There are numerous very light, highly waterproof small tents to keep you dry at night, though I have found a Vango force 10 flysheet with two sticks as tent poles works perfectly well and is roomy as well as light. No need for a groundsheet – just use a foam mat, which can always be cut up to make emergency sandals or a rucksack hipbelt pad.

Food. You're never more than five days from a shop in Europe so you don't need to carry that much food. But take stuff that is both light and filling. Noodles and tinned fish leavened with soup powder works very well. Porridge for breakfast is always welcome.

Navigation requires all the right maps, guides and a compass. For the gadget-minded you can also bring a GPS, but it isn't necessary really. Also getting lost is one of the ways to have more adventures, interact with local shepherds etc.

A good stick is psychologically often necessary, though those silly ski-pole things are somehow too serious. If you have bad knees perhaps they help, as long as you don't mind looking like a wally. An ordinary staff cut from hazel or ash is to be preferred.

Set a target number of kilometres per day. Kilometres are preferable to miles as you get more in a day that way, which gives you a boost. Don't worry about 'seeing required sights' along the way. The key is getting the distance under your belt.

The main aid to successful walking is keeping the weight of your kit down. You need one pair or trousers and one pair of shorts, three or six pairs of socks depending if you wear two pairs at a time, one jersey, one fleece or body warmer, two vests and two pairs of pants – that's for a civilised walk. For hardcore walking you have nothing but that which you wear plus a warm extra sweater, rain gear and a spare pair of socks.

Gadgets should be kept to a minimum. A multi-tool or Swiss army knife is enough. Instead of a towel I use an Arab shemagh, which can also make a handy head covering when it gets too sunny. Carry a pair of espadrilles or lightweight sandals to wear when you're not wearing boots – hardcore types just go barefoot.

A woolly hat is essential for sleeping at night and cold mornings. A flat cap also works well, but may excite derision.

Walking alone requires more determination even though it brings its own rewards. You get a chance to think about everything you have not been thinking about for years. At the end of the hike it will be as if you have serviced and spring cleaned your mind.

80 Super-advanced ultra-light backpacking

The next step after conventional backpacking is super-advanced ultra-lightweight walking. The trick is to cut everything to the bone so that you can enjoy the hike without feeling like an exhausted pack mule.

Have one change of clothes, which you wear, one spare pair of socks only and a fleece with arms you can zipper off. Wear Rohan trousers with zip-off legs so that you have trunks or shorts should you need them. Your tent and waterproof should be the same item. Get a square of waterproofed lightweight nylon (or an army basha-type flysheet) and cut a hole in the middle. Sew onto this the hood cut from an old rain coat. Liberally seal the seams with silicone cement. This can be your poncho and your tent: simply draw the hood drawstrings to seal out the rain. Make tent poles from cut branches or from your walking stick.

The only tool is a Victorinox Swiss army knife of the Mountaineer variety. For eating carve a couple of chopsticks or a wooden fork. Carry one mess tin and use this for all cooking and as your mug. Cook on fires only.

Carry a lightweight two-litre plastic water bottle. Increase that up to three or four litres if water is very scarce.

For food take only dried onions, flour, soya meat powder, noodles, soup powder and curry powder, salt, sugar and tea.

Your rucksack need only be small and light, but make sure you get one with a hip belt. Alternatively carry some gear in a big bum bag and some in a tiny nylon rucksack without a hip belt.

After three days pile all the gear into three piles: the stuff you use every day, the stuff you haven't used and the stuff you've used once. Chuck the last two piles and stride away, a lighter, and freer soul.

81 Lead men into dangerous country

Leading men on expeditions into dangerous country who are volunteers and not soldiers or employees requires you to mix authority with camaraderie or group spiritedness. There are a number of almost obvious principles, but it is surprising how often expeditions into dangerous country are led by men who fail to follow them.

The main role of the leader is to maintain momentum. On all expeditions into dangerous country there comes a point when everyone seriously considers giving up and turning back. That is your moment. That is when you keep everyone going. If you have lost your status as leader you may find you cannot pull everyone round, so to be the leader you always need to be a little isolated and a little bit self-sufficient.

1 You need to be different but equal. Naturally you have to eat the same rations as everyone else.

2 You need to do, from your own estimate, twice as much as everyone else. They will perceive this as 'doing a bit more than me'.

3 You need a permanent visual reminder of office. Otherwise you will find people encroaching on your leadership role. This could be your position: at the front when walking, helming a boat, different gear (better usually), control of navigation equipment. Trivial stuff, but leadership is primarily a social animal function (think giant silverback gorilla) not a human function.

4 Never ask for advice. If you need input, you play the chairman and ask for suggestions. You let them talk about them, but it's your decision.

5 All navigation is your job. The man who knows the way calls the shots.

6 If an expedition member is out of line and really shouldn't be there, never address another question to him again. Answer but do not ask.

7 If you need to remind the team of your independence simply eat your food away from the group.

8 You should be able to do and teach every skill required, even if you are not the best at it – though that helps.

9 If someone loses their coat give them yours. If a team believes you are always backing them up they will go along with you.

10 Before setting out outline the fact that in wild country there can only be one leader. If there is a disagreement in the field and people get heated ignore it at the time. Then at night, around the fire with a few drinks inside them, ask and get a verbal display of allegiance. Build up to it with some subtlety, though.

11 At regular intervals explain that certain decision-making moments are not helped by 'helpful suggestions'. Navigation, for example, can never be a team effort – except when looking for a landmark perhaps.

---

82 Buff your shoes to a parade gloss

Shiny shoes are scorned by some because they are considered reminiscent of the army or a law firm of yesteryear. But for those who enjoy the therapeutic feel of both cleaning and wearing highly polished shoes, here are some top tips.

Every old soldier will give you different advice, but all that means is that there is more than one way to get a super shine. The basic principle one can lose sight of is that you don't polish the leather, you polish the polish. So the main job is loading the boot or shoe with a ton of polish. The hard part is doing this in an even way.

If the boot has dimples on it use a spoon heated in a candle or gas flame to level them out, making sure that you move fast so as not to burn the leather. Before and after doing this, load the boot with polish – melt it first and apply with an old cotton T-shirt. Avoid yellow dusters as they have bits of nylon in them that scratch. For finishing off use a 'sylvet' cloth from a jewellers or silversmiths. For final buffing use a balled-up pair of tights.

The guards' method is to melt half a mess tin of beeswax into the boots first. This builds a solid base of wax. It's a 'cheat' as it replaces hours and hours of rubbing in ordinary boot wax in one go. It's also possible to shrink or burn the boots. You start by filling them, packing them hard with wet newspaper – use four papers per boot. Lace them up so that the uppers meet. Now heat them with a gas torch and melt in sticks of wax. Alternatively mix beeswax and a tin of polish in a mess tin and apply this with a cloth to the heated boot, which should suck in the mixture.

A less extreme method is to use a hairdryer to heat the leather while rubbing in shoe polish melted on the stove.

Now apply layer after layer of polish from a new tin using your sylvet cloth wrapped tightly so that it isn't wrinkly and doesn't move as you polish. Wrap your fingers in cling film first unless you want black fingers and then wrap the sylvet cloth around two or three fingers.

Dab the cloth in water you keep in the tin lid – cold water containing ice cubes works quicker than warm water. If the surface smears use more water; if it beads with water use more polish. Try and get the balance so that you get a milky greyish look. Keep going for at least an hour and prepare to be tired and sweaty. When the shine starts to appear, add a layer of dark tan or oxblood to get a nicer deeper shine. Then go back to buffing with tiny amounts of polish and a lot of water.

Another cheat is to spray and polish with 'Klear' floor polish, though this isn't waterproof. The best polish is ordinary Kiwi black polish – and new tins always work better than old ones as the solvent is important in getting the polish absorbed by the leather.

83 DIY for the cack-handed

At some stage all men fall victim to the lure of DIY. It's nice to be able to fix things and even nicer to be able to make things like tables, shelves and even chairs. For those that have never practised woodwork it may seem a difficult job, but with care and time you may be surprised at how skilled you become.

The whole secret lies in (a) the right tools and (b) extremely sharp tools.

Poor workmen may blame their tools and, hey, they ain't wrong. The right tool for the job is half the battle. Experts can bodge, but amateurs usually cock it up. You can never have too many tools. The time to buy tools is always before you need them. It's too late when you're in the middle of making a four-poster bed to discover you really do need a spokeshave or a half-size scorb – buy it now. Peruse catalogues such as those issued by Axminster tools and the Dick tool company in Germany (they have a huge selection of hand tools and sell promotional baseball caps so you can go around with 'Dick' plastered across your forehead).

Use Japanese saws from the beginning. They operate on the pull stroke not the push stroke, but apart from this they are miles sharper and cleaner to use. If you like using a hammer and chisel get Japanese chisels as they have a metal band that allows them to be hit. You have to sharpen a Japanese chisel well before using it – so refer to the sharpening section for more information (page 102). Use Japanese hammers too, as they feel much nicer in the hand.

As for power tools, it's a personal decision: I went from having lots of power tools to none and found I was quicker, as long as my chisels and saws were razor sharp. If you are making lots of the same thing then power tools are obviously faster. Sometimes, too, when you are working alone, power tools give you the odd feeling of company, back up, camaraderie. This may be nutty, but I'm sure it explains why so many amateur woodworkers have more power tools than professionals (apart from an obvious desire to appear a pro).

The other advantage of power tools is they keep working even when blunt. Although it helps to sharpen the blades on a power plane, you get away with not doing it very often – unlike on a handplane. Sharpening power tool blades is best done on a grinding wheel – another noisy machine for your workshop. Then you can get a circular saw, a bandsaw and a pillar drill just to fill up some more space. A lathe is pretty helpful, too. And don't forget a router – which is like a power drill with a blade; if you read the woodwork mags you'll find a way to do everything with a router.

The main rule for power tools is to get the best you can afford – Hitachi, deWalt, Bosch professional. Get the same tools as a professional uses and they are less likely to break or wear out. Power tools that need maintenance are a pain. Get super hard bits and blades and if you are a spendthrift get new ones rather than risk hurting yourself sharpening them.

I suppose what I'm working around to here is that DIY must be fun, it must be a blast, otherwise why do it? If power tools are your thing have fun with them; and if they are too noisy and scary and fiddly don't use them. Setting up a router can take longer than just using a chisel and a hammer.

The next thing is to use these tools. I've found the best plan is just to launch in and when you get stuck look it up in a book. But reading before you try to make something doesn't work. You have no frame of reference. Professional lute maker Alexander Hopkins made his first instrument by just copying a picture of a lute. He claimed he couldn't follow any of the textbooks he read about instrument making. The lute sounded like shaking a tin full of broken biscuits, he claimed, but he learnt enough to know what the textbooks were talking about.

Jump in, do as good a job as you can, but expect to screw it up. Persistence pays. You'll succeed second time around.

---

84 Mastery

What is mastery? How do you master a subject? How do you know when you are a master of something?

Mastery is one of the most satisfying things. Aiming for it is enough. Being a 'master' is a snare and a delusion – even if you are one. It is far better to be on the path to mastery.

The aim of mastery is simple: to get better and better at what you do, be it making meatballs or shooting a bow and arrow to sailing a boat to writing. Mastery in one area gives clues that can be used to mastering another area more quickly, but be warned, real mastery takes at least ten years of continuous, though not excessive, effort.

Are there any shortcuts to mastery? Yes, but if you are interested in them they won't work. Mostly thinking about shortcuts is a waste of time. Why? Because to achieve mastery you need to be in it for the long haul. To be in it for the long haul you had better enjoy it. Shortcuts are never ever enjoyable. If they were, everyone would use them and they wouldn't be a shortcut. An example is an intensive course in something. It'll work, but the pressure will take the fun out of it. Very often people who take intensive courses give up soon after.

Mastery is not to be taken lightly. A master craftsman is a joy to behold. He adds something to the quality of all the lives he touches. The hard part of many modern jobs is that there is no clear path to mastery, nor even much benefit to it. Being a master business executive sounds weird because it is. The whole reason to be an executive is to get on the promotion ladder to the top slot in the corporation. This is not mastery in the usual sense, more an exercise in cunning and judicious brown nosing.

Mastery is not a position, a job or a title: it is simply being very good at a demonstrable skill. The general principles of mastery are few, but here they are.

Human 'virtues' such as patience, single-mindedness and the ability to control negative emotions, are all an aid to mastery. Concentration and avoidance of distraction are another great help. The modern world revolves around increasing distraction opportunities. If you seek mastery you must actively avoid the crap distractions on offer. And even the good ones.

You must centre your life around your mastery subject. Let's say it is making models of the *Titanic* out of matchsticks. Then you must choose a job which gives you enough free time to be able to spend the best of your energy on model making. Jobs that require body and soul commitment (i.e., make you worried) are no good. They are a distraction from achieving mastery.

The plateau is the usual place to find oneself when attempting mastery. Improvements, fast or slow, are quickly taken for granted. Only when you compare yourself to how you were at the beginning do you realise how far you have come, and how far you have to go. Most of the time, then, you are trying to get better but are not significantly improving. To continue without some external sign of progress is the hardest thing. That's why you need to take it a little easy and enjoy what you are doing. The Japanese have the right approach in their martial arts. They practise every day, but they do it in such a way that it *is* just another day. Movement from the plateau is most often effected by association with someone inspiring, or a new source of interest. This produces a new perspective; it gives a new order to what you already know. Progress, beyond a certain point, is about reorganising what you already know, re-ordering it and then discovering what really is important and what isn't.

Mastery is its own reward. That's why it's such a good thing to aim for. You know when you are improving, so who cares what others think?

---

85 Stand-up comedy for the naturally nervous

Making people laugh is a noble ambition because we all need all the laughs we can get. Unfortunately in Britain, despite our much-vaunted sense of humour, we are, in public, loath to be generous to people who want to make us laugh. We despise anything that smacks of an old joke or a tired routine. What counts most of all with us is novelty or being physically scared that the comedian is about to attack us.

There are a number of strategies that will help get you started. Speak as quickly as possible and tell as many jokes or funny stories in your allotted time as you can. Have a massive surfeit of material and overwhelm the audience, giving them no chance to heckle and break in. This is the Ben Elton method.

Go up assuming that what you are delivering is a serious speech in a certain persona and that any laughter is a kind of affront. This is the Andy Kaufman method.

Search the audience for the weakest and least offensive

person and mercilessly pick on them, direct the innate viciousness of the comedy crowd at the poor sod. The fear that you may then turn on them will make the audience laugh with uneasy complicity.

The main thing is to have a strategy that allows you to bound onto that stage as if you were born there, own it and have the right to be there more than anyone else. Showmanship, which is success in front of an audience, is less about talent and more about projecting unrelenting confidence. Even if the role you play is of someone timid, you must be fantastically assured in your timidity.

The crowd meanwhile have an animal sixth sense about confidence and will aim to shake you of it in the way a dog worries away at a bone.

Employ counter-intuitive moves. If the audience doesn't respond the usual tactic is to relent, be more ingratiating, more timid; we want to fit in and that's how you fit in to a group, by fading into the woodwork. But on stage the spotlight is only on you. There is nowhere to hide. So do the opposite. When they don't laugh, give it more energy, more push, more brass neck. Just as singers know the cure for going out of tune is more energy not less, so the comedian needs to project more energy to subdue that slavering crowd of drunks and nay-saying know-alls.

Subject matter. Find a subject you like talking about in civilian life, a subject in which you are sincerely interested and that sincerity, if pushed to the fore, becomes the touchstone of your humour. Let's say you have a passionate belief in using natural nappies for the newly born. Use your sincere interest in nappies and post-natal care to illuminate all that is funny about the subject. Or let us say you love talking about the *Flashing Blade* and *Belle and Sebastian* (not the band, the 1960s French TV programme); you can put it under the kind of scrutiny that turns it into ripe comedy. If you can fake or are genuinely sincere in your interest the humour will come.

If your own delivery and persona seems unfunny, perform your whole act as someone else. Pretend you're an aging, drug-obsessed, failed rock star with all kinds of medical problems.

The tighter you focus on some area, the more funny ideas it will generate. It can be hard to make ten jokes up about your life unless you are naturally risible. Focus instead on the moments between waking and eating breakfast, and the ideas will come much faster. Making up jokes about your body and its failings is harder than thinking up a routine based around your feet, or even your big toe.

Novelty is key. Comedians have been doing observational humour about their lives for years. Why not go in for the opposite and do jokes based on the ancient Greeks? Instead of finding humour in TV commercials, politicians and current events, make up funny stuff about your favourite crustaceans, eating caviar or the sex life of the Inuit. Most comedians, though clever and inventive, lack breadth of information. Mine obscure areas that have never been mined before. And overproduce – you can never have too much material. The more you have the more you can afford to get rid of the stuff that isn't funny.

Accumulate material that gets you bubbling over with excitement, even if that isn't the way you deliver it. You need that kind of energy to 'sell' the audience on you. People buy energy when it comes down to it and if you can sell them some they'll be happy.

Practise long and hard in front of the bathroom mirror where the acoustics are better. Note the weakest parts: these are the bits you mentally want to hurry through. Add more and better laughs to these sections and note the new weakest parts. When the bit you thought was your funniest stuff at the beginning seems weak you are ready to perform – in front of friends. Just insinuate parts of your routine into everyday conversation or sessions in the pub. Expect a few hiccups and backfires even at this stage, but gradually you'll have road tested the lot before you go on stage.

Spontaneity is actually just the result of rehearsal time. Just as a jazz musician is really putting bits together that he's already worked on – but not in that order – so a spontaneous exchange is a reworking or substitution of something already rehearsed.

If you are word perfect you will have the confidence to depart from the script. If you attempt to wing it, you'll be in trouble at the first sign of any adverse reaction from the audience.

As a final test before performing, video yourself at home. The shock of seeing yourself perform on video may be the biggest teaching aid of all.

The opening is always the hardest bit – that's when you win or lose them. Never ever ask: 'Hi, how you doing? Having a good night?' You've lost already. Dean Martin's routine was to walk on, stand at the mike, take a puff of a cigarette, drink a bit of his drink, look at the audience, pause, then walk over to the pianist and ask: 'How long have I been on?'

Decide on your heckler strategy before you go on stage. Have ten good heckler killers and use them without thought – get them mixed up as a joke on the fact that you have pre-worked out heckler killers.

If you find yourself in a position where you aren't getting many laughs never demand them. Simply increase your energy of delivery and slow down your delivery rate. Slower and slower until you get the feeling that the audience are willing you to speed up. Put in a long pause after a punch line. Lead them to it. Watch how Steve Martin turns something very ordinary into a laugh by the way he underlines it with a pause.

---

86 Dealing with unexploded bombs

While out in a foreign country you may chance upon unexploded ordnance. Leave well alone, naturally. Should you find yourself in a minefield, don't panic: the front line infantry in the Battle of El Alamein crossed German minefields *before* the sappers cleared them. And their only tool of detection was a long-bladed bayonet. Even today the bayonet or knife blade is still the method used by infantry caught unawares in a minefield.

If there are tracks across the minefield walk or drive in them. If you can backtrack in your own footprints, do so. Otherwise gently probe the ground in front of you – the slight touch of a blade will not set off a mine, only your weight will do that. Watch out for trip wires that extend from mines, though these are less likely in an old and forgotten minefield. Check by probing with a smaller knife *under* mines, especially anti-tank mines, for a grenade primed to go off if you lift the mine out. Moving forward lying prone will reduce pressure on any mine, but visibility is reduced and accidental movements become less controllable. If you do discover a mine, either remove it with care or mark it with a pair of crossed sticks and move around it.

Letter bombs do not always signal their arrival with a ticking clock. You can put enough C4 in a jiffy bag or an old Amazon book carton to kill the recipient. The secret is not to open things you have not ordered or asked for. If you are undecided there are ways of opening a letter bomb that are safer than others. To handle the knocks and disturbances of the mail system a letter bomb cannot be fragile, otherwise it would have exploded in the letterbox when it was posted. The trigger will never be shock-based; it will always be some kind of release mechanism triggered by opening the package. The simplest is a piece of clock spring as a contact held together if it's shorting the circuit, or apart if it is simple contact. Reducing pressure on this sets off the bomb. These pressure switches can be at either end of the package or at the front and back. They won't be at the corners. Use a pair of shears or strong scissors to cut off the tip of the corner – then take a look inside. Semtex is odourless, but homemade and other plastic explosives can smell of almonds. If you glimpse wires, don't cut them as they may be part of a short circuit. Attach broom handles by wire and tape to a pair of long-handled hedge cutters. Cover the bomb with sandbags leaving a narrow gap for the shears. Shelter behind a low wall with just your hands showing, ideally in welding gauntlets. Chomp through the wires. A cruel but effective way to check if something is a letter bomb is to feed it to goats in a remote field.

---

87 Making moonshine with a wok

Be warned! People in less-enlightened countries where moonshine is frowned upon by customs and excise should do their moonshining while on holiday in New Zealand and Croatia, where home distilling is legal.

Moonshine can be poisonous if it is made in the old backwoods way using a car radiator as a distilling coil. This can add lead, not to mention anti-freeze, to the brew, which even hardened drinkers may find hard to stomach.

Other dangers much touted in moonshining circles include the poisonous effect of methanol on humans – namely blindness and death from ingesting as little as 100ml of it. If you distil using the old car radiator or a commercially available still bought on holiday, or your own still made by plumbing a copper pipe into the top of a pressure cooker, you should discard the first 50ml or so of moonshine. Since methanol evaporates at 64.7°C and ethanol at 78.4°C, almost all of the methanol will be in the first drops of distillate.

The second way to avoid excess methanol is to make your base alcohol from sugar not starch-laden products. Avoid spuds, corn and barley and brew from pure sugar, molasses, grapes and other fruits. If you use peaches and plums remove the stones, as these contain cyanide that is concentrated by distillation.

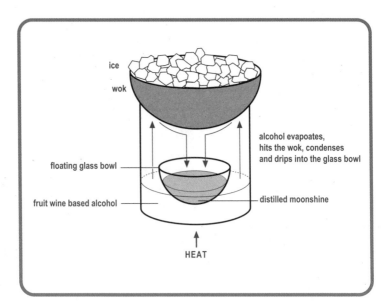

Make your base alcohol as if making wine but include the fruit pulp. Typical moonshine can be made from orange juice, sugar and brewer's yeast. A better flavour can be obtained from 2kg of fresh fruit to 5 litres of water. Mature it in a 20-litre plastic beer-brewing bucket. After ten days it should be ready for 'shining'. Make sure it hasn't gone bad, as this will increase the methanol level.

For those intent on making a still – which is legal as long as it isn't used to distil booze – then remove the central valve out of an old non-aluminium pressure cooker, fix by general bodgery and maybe some rad weld, a plumbing attachment for a piece of copper pipe (bits available at your local DIY store), and then add a length of copper tube bent in a loop which you pass under a slow-running tap in the sink. The distillate drips out the other end.

Assuming you have not converted a pressure cooker into a still then assemble a wok, a big cylindrical pot, and a glass bowl. That's all you need to start producing fruit-based alcohol stronger than anything you can buy at Oddbins.

Place your fruit wine based alcohol in the biggest flat-bottomed cylindrical pot you have. Floating in it you put a glass bowl which doesn't touch the sides of the pot. On top you put the wok with a well-cleaned bottom. A curved-bottomed wok works better than a flat-bottomed one. Inside the wok put ice cubes and water.

The principle is devilishly simple: you heat the alcohol base until the ethanol evaporates. When it hits the cold wok bottom it condenses and dribbles to the lowest part of the wok where it drips off into the bowl (see diagram).

Keep it on a low boil so that bubbling and froth don't pollute your brandy or schnapps. Don't let the bowl touch the bottom of the pot either. Keep your wok topped up with ice cubes.

The harmful methanol, because of its lower boiling temperature, escapes out of the sides of the wok. This is because the bowl will be above the temperature that evaporates methanol. Any left in the bowl will be boiled off harmlessly and will end up in your kitchen atmosphere. But beware of wok distilling a high methanol-content brew, such as beer or potato wine or a fruit wine that has gone off.

After a goodly while you retrieve the bowl wearing gloves as it will be hot. You also need enough room between the bowl and the pot to get your fingers down. The bowl contains your moonshine! Rent or buy the DVD of *Deliverance* and see what generations of imbibing moonshine does to your sex drive.

---

88 Any port in a storm

Port is a great drink to take while travelling in hot countries. It does not require cooling like beer and white wine, it is stronger than red wine, but not as brutal as pure spirits. Port should be stored with label uppermost, which is the way to hold it when decanting. This has to be done before drinking. If you plan on taking your port abroad, you can decant it in rough conditions through several layers of tissue or kitchen roll. Ruby port is better for travelling as it is younger and has very little sediment.

Port is always passed from right to left. To leave the port bottle in front of you, even when seated cross legged in the jungle, is considered hogging. Keep the bottle moving and don't deprive others of their tipple.

---

89 Croc knowledge

Crocs can be caught best at night by shining a torch in their eyes, sneaking up and dropping a cloth over their faces to stop them from seeing. When they can't see they don't resist. This is ancient knowledge – in the fifth century BC Herodotus speaks of catching crocodiles by covering their eyes with mud.

Once its eyes are covered, if you are a Steve Irwin-type, jump down and wrestle the thing. Otherwise, hook a rope loop around its snout and bind it fast. For very big crocs you can use a nylon tape with a ratchet tie-down (a lightweight version of the kind used to secure lorry loads). Crocs have very powerful shutting muscles, but their mouth opening muscles are easily overcome. Use other tie-downs or rope to secure the croc to a long carrying pole.

If your aim is simply to escape from a croc belting after you, bear in mind that crocs are very fast – but only in a straight line. Sudden changes of direction confuse it and take a while for it to follow. Exit fast in a zig-zag fashion.

Caught by a croc in the water your main worry is to avoid being drowned rather than eaten. The croc will aim to hold you underwater until you stop struggling. Stabbing its eyes out with a sharp knife may distract it enough for you to break free.

90 Recognise fake diamonds

Diamonds are always welcome gifts – except when they are fake. Breathe on it for a quick test: if it clouds over it's probably glass or zirconite, as diamond has a higher specific heat value and will remain clear. Drop it in water and you may observe a join line appear between the tiny top and the more substantial bottom. This is an old trick – the tiny top diamond is used to scratch glass or a Moh's hardness scale while the glued-on glass bottom is ignored. Water has a strong refractive effect on light and this helps show up any joins.

Diamonds are not called sparklers for nothing. Hold a diamond at arms' length and look at it horizontally. Then tilt it slowly. If you can see through the stone it's probably false: a real diamond sparkles so brightly you won't be able to see through it.

91 Teach a bear to dance

Short of a new skill to attract the crowds while busking at Covent Garden? Teach a bear to dance. Don't get a grizzly or an American black bear – see the bear-charging section for why (page 47). A more timid and amenable European bear is best, either from the Russian Caucasus, Greek Pindus or the Balkans. You need a bear cub, preferably one that has yet to be weaned. Feed it daily with a warm bottle of milk and it will become attached to you and trust you.

Start playing music and holding its paws as soon as it can

stand. Dance yourself so it gets the basic idea. Bears prefer upbeat music so steer clear of Nirvana or Slipknot. Only do this in short spells and reward the bear with chocolate and other goodies after each dance session.

After a while the bear will get up on its hind legs and dance without you holding its paws. Immediately reward it for this. From then on it only gets its praise and chocolate when it dances standing up on its hind legs alone.

If the bear gets too eager and starts dancing without music don't reward it as things could get out of hand. The idea is to reinforce dancing activity only.

When performing with your bear, be prepared to run away if you see the RSPCA or the police. Reward the bear for being a good sprinter, too.

92 Secret writing

If you have been banged up for whatever reason you may have need of an invisible ink. The easiest to use is milk. Write between the lines of an ordinary missive (usually the best strategy with all invisible inks). The recipient need only smear a dirty finger over the writing for it to show up.

More devious methods include writing with urine, which shows up as you hold the paper over a flame. More powerfully you can mix cobalt chloride (one part), gum arabic (one part) and water (eight parts), which shows up nicely blue when the paper is heated.

To make something show up as green when the paper is heated, mix equal parts of nickel and cobalt chloride with five times as much water.

Rice water left over from boiling the stuff will show up if the letter is lightly brushed with iodine.

93 The correct etiquette for emails

There is no correct etiquette for emails. People develop their own style. Some stick to it religiously, but then it can feel awkward if someone else's style is radically different. Then there is the mental tussle of whose style will dominate. Will the man who started with a 'Dear Mr Twigger' receive a dear in return or the ubiquitous and somehow uncool 'Hi'. There are those who inject a kind of urgency with the name Rob: and then the colon. I have tried 'Dude', 'Yo' and 'Hey' a number of times. The simple 'Hello' is ultra English and too straight a bat if you ask me.

Then there is the signing off. 'Yours' and 'yours sincerely' just won't work except in faux letters to officials. There seems to be a greeting card culture of 'best wishes', 'regards', 'best regards' etc. I know one guy who sticks to regards through thick and thin – the good part of that is that 'regards' covers all bases. However, once you get warmer and do a 'cheers' or an 'all the best' then you cannot go back to 'regards' without looking as though you're being frosty. There are many and varied degrees of frost in emails that are entirely absent in phonecalls and letters. It is almost as if this form of communication is reluctant and therefore draws out our worst side. Anyway. 'Cheers' always looks faintly clumsy. Blokes like it. Never seen 'au revoir' – but that might work, as would 'adios'. 'See you soon' is OK if true, if not silly. 'Speak soon' likewise. 'ATB' as a nice abbreviation of all the best would run I reckon. 'Be well' is one I like – American and a tad over familiar yet pretending interest so overcoming those charges, although it may be a bit international. 'Many salaams' is one I have yet to see in common usage.

94 Ice-hole swimming

There is no better and quicker way to face the demons that insist you are more wimp than warrior than to take a quick dip in an ice hole. Preferably one that is full of water – water that will be no more than a few degrees above zero and, if seawater, even a degree or two lower than zero. Is it dangerous? Only if you go into shock, stay in the water too long or forget to remove your trunks when you emerge into the sub-zero air.

Despite old people in Finland and Russia water bombing into icy ponds, first timers can go into shock. Lowering yourself in is the recommended way to enter icy water – down a ladder or steps cut at the side of the hole. Wear a woolly hat and don't get your head underwater is a good way to start out. Wet hair can start freezing immediately and suck the warmth out of you in seconds. Once in the water, your first reaction will be extreme breathlessness, literally gasping at the cold of it. Deliberately breathe out a little longer than normal to control this involuntary reaction. Stay in the water no more than a minute for your first dip – over time you can extend this. Expect, even in this short time, to start shivering and tingling all over.

When you emerge dripping onto the surrounding snow the chances are the air temperature will be much lower than the water temperature. Now you face the twin perils of light-headed delirium brought on by your sudden immersion and frozen swimwear. The delirium can be your undoing. You may not even feel cold anymore – a sure sign that your core body temperature is plummeting. If you don't strip everything wet off immediately and swathe yourself in warm towels, your swimming trunks will start turning to cardboard and freezing to your testicles – definitely something to be avoided.